D1825147

LESS THAN A YEAR TO LIVE

DR. KELLY ZACHARY-ARNOLD

WESTBOW
PRESS®
A DIVISION OF THOMAS NELSON
& ZONDERVAN

Scripture taken from the King James Version of the Bible.

Scripture taken from the New King James Version®. Copyright © 1982 by Thomas Nelson. Used by permission. All rights reserved.

Scripture quotations marked (NIV) are taken from the Holy Bible, New International Version®, NIV®. Copyright © 1973, 1978, 1984, 2011 by Biblica, Inc.™ Used by permission of Zondervan. All rights reserved worldwide. www.zondervan.com The "NIV" and "New International Version" are trademarks registered in the United States Patent and Trademark Office by Biblica, Inc.™

Scriptures marked GW are taken from the GOD'S WORD (GW): Scripture taken from GOD'S WORD® copyright © 1995 by God's Word to the Nations. All rights reserved.

WestBow Press books may be ordered through booksellers or by contacting:

WestBow Press
A Division of Thomas Nelson & Zondervan
1663 Liberty Drive
Bloomington, IN 47403
www.westbowpress.com
1 (866) 928-1240

ISBN: 978-1-9736-3541-3 (sc)
ISBN: 978-1-9736-3540-6 (hc)
ISBN: 978-1-9736-3542-0 (e)

Library of Congress Control Number: 2018908913

Print information available on the last page.

WestBow Press rev. date: 08/17/2018

CONTENTS

Thanks to my God, Who loved me so much that He sent His only Son, Jesus, to die on the cross to take away my sins, and by Whose stripes I was healed. I give You all the glory, honor and praise. I am alive today because of You, and I will spend the rest of my life telling the world of your incredible grace and mercy.

ACKNOWLEDGEMENTS

Thanks to my publisher, Eric Schroeder, for encouraging me, praying for me, going to bat for me…holding my hand. Eric, I couldn't have done this without you. You are more than my publisher, you are my friend.

Thanks to Pastor Todd Rigney and Missy Price Rigney for serving as our pastors, but also for always being there when I needed advice, spiritual guidance and a friend or a shoulder to cry on.

Thanks to Jason Crabb. Your music inspired, encouraged, uplifted and drew Ron close to God during the worst time in his life. Your music allowed him to walk "Through the Fire."

Thanks to Bob Lubell, for inviting me to be filmed for his Internet Video Ministry, ComeOnLetsGo.com Bob, you shared my testimony with millions of people all over this world. Thank you for your ministry and for spreading the news of God's grace and mercy to those who may never have a chance to hear it otherwise. Thanks for all your help and for being such a great friend.

Thanks to Lisa and Ed Gordon. First our neighbors, then our dear friends. Lisa, you provided us with love and many home cooked meals when I was unable to cook. You have become so dear to us. We appreciate and love you guys.

Thanks to Marine David Dahn. David, you made my husband the "Duck" laugh when he should have been crying. You had his "six" and I knew I could count on you. You and your wife Carol are so special to us. We thank you for your prayers and support. You showed what a real man is all about. For a "Naval Reject", you are something else. Thanks for all the laughs! Semper Fi!

Thanks to our Shreveport "family" Charlie and Janie Jones- our neighbors and adopted family, along with Dan and Peggy Tilton and the rest of the Tilton Clan. You took us in and loved us and made us not only a part of your Church family, but your adopted family, as well. Janie, thanks for the best coffee ever. Charlie went home to Jesus on July 4, 2018. He celebrated the ultimate freedom-his way.

Thanks to Karen, my favorite nurse. You are so special to me. You stayed with me while I cried and held my hand.

Thanks to all my friends and family, including my FB friends who were always there for me, loving me, encouraging me and praying for me.

A special thanks to Mimi, our Bichon Frise, and Mason, our Neapolitan Mastiff, who were at my feet for every word I wrote. Even at 3:00 in the morning, when they were tired and wanted to go to bed, they stayed with me. The heartbeats at my feet.

Our heartfelt thanks to Ed and Lisa Gordon who designed and produced the beautiful Cover Photo.

DEDICATION PAGE

To my darling husband, Dr. Ron Arnold. You took care of me, did the cooking, cleaning, shopping and never once complained. You held your pain inside and only told God you fears and terrors while watching your wife die, but that gave you a closer walk with God. I don't know how to tell you thank you for all you did. You are my husband, my lover, my best friend, my soul mate. I love you with all my heart, my darling Ronbo.

To my precious mother, Shirley Chromeenes Zachary, who dedicated her life to make sure I was thoroughly loved and raised in Church three times a week. She was the greatest Christian I've ever known. Mom, I am who I am today because of you.

To Pastors Jerry and Ann Price. I fell in love with your family when I was just an "ornery" teenager. You were my example of a Christian husband and wife. This love spanned 40 years and when I needed someone to pray for me, I went to you. As a teenager, I played the piano as you sang "How can I say thanks for the things You have done for me? Things so undeserved, yet You gave to prove your love for me. The voices of a million angels cannot express my gratitude. All that I am, and ever hope to be- I owe it all to Thee." This is now my theme song. I love you with all my heart, and you're right. We are family.

To Jesse Grantham, whose prayer to God was answered by my healing. Jesse, you moved mountains for me, held my hand and showed this little "Squidley" your integrity, generosity, and immense love of God. Thank you for being the man and Christian that you are.

To Sister Angie Shaughnessy, you saw something in me that no one else did. You saw beyond my bravado and saw a hurt little girl who needed someone to talk to. You taught me to write, you taught me the love of the written word, you taught me to love learning. I became the student I was because of your love and insight. I love you Sister Angie. Thank you for rescuing me.

To my children, Brittany Elizabeth, Brianna Victoria and Anthony Tyler, who make up my heart.

FORWARD FOR KELLY'S BOOK

Ann and I are so grateful that God allowed us to be a part of this irrefutable miracle. In this great testimony you will see how God steps into an impossible situation and instantly changes everything. The "what" question is answered and you will see there is no debate that God has done an instantaneous miracle that cannot be explained by natural laws or denied by the medical field. I always thank God for the wonderful world He created that now cries out for the return of Christ (Romans 8: 22) but I believe this miracle has a wondrous purpose.

The question that comes to mind is what would that purpose be? God doesn't give these kinds of miracles to entertain the curiosity of people. Miracles are not given to increase the faith of believers. We know that real faith comes by "hearing the Word of God." (Romans 10:17) Why is this true? Because the Bible is a revelation of God! And the more you realize who God is and His heart toward you, the more your faith will increase. God wants you to know Him and His purpose for you. He is the Mighty healer! He heals emotionally, physically and spiritually and God is able. As the scripture says, "A bruised reed He will not break". God has a tremendous desire to make us whole and complete no matter where we are or what got us there! Look to our Gracious God! We cannot have true healing without the Healer.

Throughout the Old Testament and the New Testament, people saw miracles of God. There seems to me to be one common tread! God was revealing Himself to people who did not know Him. In many cases He was showing that He is the only true and living God!

He showed Himself to Pharaoh and Egypt during the 10 plagues that addressed Egypt's false gods!

He Showed Himself to King Nebuchadnezzar and Babylon when God delivered Daniel from the Lions and Daniel's three comrades, Shadrach, Meshach and Abednego delivering them from the fiery furnace.

Daniel 6:20 (GW)
[20] As he came near the den where Daniel was, the king called to Daniel with anguish in his voice, "Daniel, servant of the living God! Was God, whom you always worship, able to save you from the lions?" Daniel cries out from the lion pit, Yes He's Able and I'm Here!

Daniel 3:15 (GW)
If you don't worship it (The idol god), you will immediately be thrown into a blazing furnace. What god can save you from my power then?" When the three comrades came out without even the smell of smoke on them, the King said, in **Daniel 3:28 (GW)** [28] Nebuchadnezzar said, "Praise the God of Shadrach, Meshach, and Abednego. He sent his angel and saved his servants, who trusted him…"

The miracle you will read about in this book God anointed Kelly to write, will show you and people who do not know God, that God is real, powerful and loving. You will want to share this book with people you love and care about. God is revealing Himself to this generation before His return.

I encourage you to read this book with an open heart.

REMEMBER: IT'S NOT THE SIZE OF YOUR FAITH, IT'S THE SIZE OF YOUR GOD!

Pastor Jerry Price

PROLOGUE

The day had started out like every other day.

Ron had gone to work early that morning and I had slept in. That is, until the dogs decided it was time for me to get up and ganged up on me! Try telling a 200-pound Mastiff that you want to go back to sleep. It doesn't work.

It was a beautiful day in Shreveport, and I was fortunate that I didn't have to walk the dogs. I just opened the French doors leading to the backyard and let them have the freedom to run as they pleased. Mason was barking as we heard the sounds of our neighbor working in her backyard. It was a day that made you happy to be alive. The flowers were in bloom, birds were flying from tree to tree, and Mason was digging up a flowerbed for the hundredth time. I could see the dirt flying through the air before it landed on the patio. He was never going to outgrow his puppyhood!

I gathered up what I was going to need to camp out on the sofa in the den. Water, cell phone, glasses, T.V. remote and my Bible. I was all settled in when our 18-pound Bichon Frise, Mimi, came in from the backyard. She was fed up with her "little" brother chasing her, so she sought refuge among my blankets.

I had spent time talking with God and thanking Him again for His infinite wisdom in caring for Ron and me. I knew if anything should happen to me, Ron would have a lot of "family" looking out for him.

I felt like we were in heaven, living in our neighborhood. My neighbor, Janie, had already called me, as usual, to check on me and see if I wanted to come over for coffee or if I needed anything. I was tired and not quite up to visiting, but we chatted on the phone for a long time.

After I hung up from Janie, I was thinking about how blessed we were. God had given us a home right in the middle of the "Promised Land." Janie, Charlie and all their vast family had taken a couple of "orphans" and adopted us, nurtured us and loved us. What more could we ask for? Even though my heart was getting bad, I was convinced that the doctors in this area would be able to diagnose me, and I could get my life back. I felt so fortunate to have found a doctor that took me seriously. All I had to do was tell him one time that my heart wasn't acting right, and he got me the help I needed. I didn't like wearing the Holter monitor for a week, but at this point, I would do anything to find out what was wrong and get it fixed!

I was trying to figure out what would be easy to fix for dinner when the telephone rang. It was the nurse at my cardiologist's office. I had turned in the Holter monitor two days before. "Dr. Zachary-Arnold, we've been trying to get in touch with you. The doctor needs you to come in right away!"

I immediately went into denial mode, "What day do you want me to come in?" In my mind, I was thinking, "Oh, this can't be good."

She said, "The doctor wants you to come in now. Right now!"

I have made a career of studying human behavior, and I can read a person's voice almost as well as I can read their facial expressions. From the tone and urgency of her voice, I went from denial mode to panic mode. I wanted my husband. I needed Ron! I grabbed my phone from where I had dropped it in shock. With trembling fingers, I scrolled though the contacts until I saw the face that I loved so passionately. *"Please, God, let him answer the phone!"*

I was shaking as I called my husband, Ron, at work. "Honey, the doctor's office just called, and they want me to come in right away!" I was trying not to panic, but he could hear it in my voice.

"I'm leaving right now to pick you up." I could hear the tension in his voice. The voice that was so dear to me sounded scared. *Please, Ron, don't sound like this! I need you to tell me that everything is going to be fine. You're my rock. You can't be afraid. I depend on you!*

After several years of having heart problems and no diagnosis, it was with mixed feelings I threw on some clothes and waited for "Ronbo." While I waited I was praying, *"Okay, God, we have been praying that someone would be able to find out what was wrong with my heart and apparently, they have, and to be honest... I'm scared. Give me the strength and grace to face this and give the doctors the wisdom in treating this."*

My husband of only five years arrived to get me. I could tell he was worried, because when he gets like that, he becomes very businesslike. I was looking for my purse, and he snapped, "You don't need your purse, let's just go!" *Okay, Ronbo… let's get this over with.*

Ron drove like I was in labor and ready to deliver any minute! He was trying to reassure me, "This is probably nothing. You just need a pacemaker, and then you will be fine." He kept repeating this. He was trying to reassure himself as much as he was me, but I could see the terror on his face.

We were ushered back into an exam room, and it wasn't two minutes before the doctor walked in. I could immediately tell from the look on his face that this did not bode well for us, and the hair on the back of my neck stood up. "I got the results of your Holter monitor, and I don't like what I'm seeing on your printout. For one thing, you've had a heart attack."

The bottom dropped out from under me. Wait a minute, this was not what I was expecting to hear. *"No, God, not a heart attack! I've prayed to You about this. It's just a problem with my heart rhythm, remember? I just need a simple pacemaker, and I'll be good as new!"*

The voice of the doctor penetrated the haze of my fear, "I'm scheduling you for a Stress Echocardiogram right away to see what is going on." A Stress Echo is a Stress Test with an Echocardiogram done within seconds of the test.

The nurse came back into our room with the appointment day and time. It was the next day! I was still trying to wrap my head around my heart attack, and now they want to do a Stress Echo tomorrow? I panicked and started telling them that that was too soon, and my day was already scheduled. The doctor said that he had rearranged his schedule to do this tomorrow. Then the *voice of authority* chimed in, "Kel, you *are* going to do this tomorrow." Now I feel like I'm being ganged up on. The doctor, nurse and now my husband had made the decision for me. I was outnumbered, and I didn't like it at all. I had the irrational thought that if I could just turn and run from the room, everything would go back to the way it was before I had walked into the doctor's office.

I had tears running down my face. Ron took me into his arms, and I began to sob. I'd had a heart attack, and the doctor suspected something else was going on. He wasn't saying anything, and I wasn't asking. I just wanted to go home and crawl in bed and cry. We left the doctor's office in a fog. Later on, I thought about the bad night I had recently on March 21, 2016, with the chest pain and trouble breathing, and I knew that was when I had the heart attack. I didn't realize it at the time, but my heart rate had dropped from 118 beats per minute (bpm) to 30 bpm. 30 bpm is not compatible with sustaining life. I don't know how I survived, except that God had His Hand on me. I should have called 911 that night, but that isn't how I do things. I wait until I don't have any other choice before I seek medical help.

It was later that I realized that, for once in my life, I had not drilled the doctor on what he thought was going on, or what he was looking for. I have always tended to practice "backseat medicine." I walk into a doctor's office, and I give him my diagnosis and then wait for his "second opinion."

On the ride home, we didn't say much. I saw Ron wiping away tears. I had tears streaming down my face. "God, I can't do this! Where are you? I need you. Please help me!"

We walked like zombies into our beautiful home. Mimi and Mason came to greet us, and they could tell something was wrong. I knelt down and they began to lick away my tears, which made me cry even harder. I went into our bedroom and crawled into bed and sobbed. What just happened? It wasn't supposed to be like this. I was just going to get a pacemaker for an arrhythmia disorder! I don't remember the rest of that day. I just remember thinking that I had not planned for this. *"God, this isn't how we discussed this. Remember? I was just having an arrhythmia disorder that could be cured with a pacemaker!"*

1

HOW IT ALL BEGAN

I don't remember when I became a Christian. I grew up in the Church of God and Assembly of God churches all my life. My mother was the church pianist, and when I got older I played the piano for the choir and for special singing. We went to church three times a week for as long as I could remember.

When I got in my early twenties, I became a backslider much to my mom's distress. Instead of going to church, I was training in the martial art of Tae Kwon Do and earning my Black Belt Degree. I decided it was more fun to train, compete with my friends and end a grueling competition by going to a party. I wasn't a bad person, but I certainly couldn't call myself a Christian either. All this time I was plagued with guilt. I knew what I was doing was wrong, but it takes a lot to get through my thick head. So, it was no surprise to my mother when I met a man who wasn't a Christian and married him. Three children later we got divorced; it was time to get serious with my life.

I needed to find the Lord again. My life had not turned out like I had wanted, and it was time to make changes. I had gone to college before, but I had not applied myself. Now, I was a divorced mother of three children, and it was time to go back to my roots—roots that were firmly ensconced in God! I first had to humble myself before the God of all creation and ask for forgiveness. That was the easy part. He embraced me as the Prodigal, and I once again fell in love with Him. He was my Savior, and I would never stray again. Now, the education part wasn't going to be as easy.

The downside to growing up as a Navy brat is that you don't have continuity of education. I had gone to so many schools I couldn't even remember the names! It also has a detrimental effect on self-confidence. I was always the new kid on the block, and I became very self-conscious. So, to over compensate, I became a clown with my fellow students and my teachers.

I managed to successfully struggle through my studies, except for math. That was the one subject I could not get. I managed to get D's in math, but I think they just passed me along out of sympathy. I didn't know it at the time, since it was yet to be discovered, but I had Attention Deficit Disorder minus the hyperactivity. I remember once thinking in algebra class as the teacher was trying to explain a concept to me, *I'm trying, but I just can't get it to click in my mind!*

"Kelly, Sister Mary Elizabeth wants to see you in her office." Those words struck terror in my heart! Sister Mary Elizabeth, a nun, was the principal at St. Mary's Academy, where I attended high school. With fear and trepidation, I went into her office. "Kelly, we have to talk. You are failing all of your classes, but you have a very high I.Q. You just aren't applying yourself and trying hard enough."

I didn't have the nerve to tell Sister Mary Elizabeth that there was so much more to me than people knew. For one thing, my father was an abusive alcoholic and I didn't have the best home life to nurture a struggling student. Secondly, I knew I had a learning disability, but I couldn't describe it. I did try, but I couldn't get things figured out in my brain. I left her office feeling discouraged. Little did I know, but I was about to find someone who believed in me.

Sister Angie was my homeroom and English teacher. She saw something in me that no one else did. She was young, beautiful and very popular to all her students. She sat down with me and said, "Kelly, I know you have it in you to be a better student."

We spoke at length, and I left feeling like I had someone who understood me. She had all her students begin a journal for class, and it was there that I learned to write. More importantly, I had found someone I could pour out my heart. For extra credit, she would allow us to turn in the journal more often. I looked forward to picking up my journal, because Sister Angie didn't just read my journal, she wrote back to me. She was my counselor, my friend, and someone I could tell about my father. It was then that I began to apply myself to my studies, and my grades improved, except for algebra. The thought of going to that class stuck terror in my heart. I *just* couldn't get it! I managed to pass high school, just barely. But Sister Angie had planted a seed that would blossom the rest of my life. We recently reconnected, and I told her that I owed so much to her.

After my divorce, Mom invited me to live with her while I went back to school to study forensic medicine. But first I was going to have to learn algebra. Mom and I went to Barnes and Noble and I found several self-study books on algebra, and I tackled them with a tenacity I had never had before. Much to my surprise, I found out that not only was I good at algebra, but I *loved* it! I loved every minute of it! I became so proficient at it, that I was awarded a scholarship after I took my college entrance exam. In college, I excelled at all my studies, including getting three bachelor's degrees in six years. I was hooked on education!

Through all my accomplishments, awards and Honor Society, I am sorry to say that I never once gave the glory to God. I thought there was nothing I couldn't do, but I never stopped to reflect on the fact that all that I was, and all that I had done was due to the Lord. It had taken me reaching rock bottom to call out to my Heavenly Father. I was so ashamed. The first time I walked back into church, I fell to my knees, crying as if my heart was broken. It was then I saw the grace and mercy of a loving God. I came to know Him in an intimate way and learned to rely on Him for everything. Little did I know that I was about to have my faith tested through the fire.

On October 6, 2007, my beloved mother went home to Jesus. I have never met a stronger or better example of a Christian. She never stopped praying for me while I was straying. She was my best friend and the years I lived with her were such a blessing. Even though we lived together, she still called me six or seven times a day on my cell! She was sweet, funny, adventurous, and everyone loved her. Her death devastated me, and there were times I really didn't think I could go on without her. I still find myself picking up my phone to call her, ten years later. But, I have the reassurance that I will see her again.

It was during this time that I began to have severe tachycardia, especially at night. As soon as I would lie down, my heart started pounding and skipping beats. The only thing that helped was for me to get out of bed. I was mourning the loss of my mom like I was five- years old. Mom and I had had a unique and wonderful relationship. Even at my age, if I was having a bad day, I would put my head on her shoulder or lie with my head in her lap while she rubbed my back. She knew how hard I was pushing myself, and she was my biggest fan. I could talk to Mom about anything. After her death, I didn't want anyone else. I pushed all my friends away when they tried to help. I just wanted Mom back. My heart was broken, and it was letting me know. The fast heart rate kept me from sleeping, and I was worn out.

I was angry at God. I cried and screamed at Him. *"How could You do this to me? Why did You have to take my mom away from me?!"* I was even angry at my mother for dying, and I screamed at her as well. *"Why did you leave me? I can't live without you! Why did you have to die?"* I know that my thoughts and feelings were not rational, but they are a natural part of the grieving process. I needed someone to yell at. Fortunately, God has very broad shoulders and a kind and loving heart. I'm sure He grieved with me, and was thinking, *"My child I am with you and I will never forsake you."*

When I look back at my life, I can see how God was always there, even when I couldn't feel Him. As a little girl of eight-years old, God revealed His power and love for me. This has sustained me through some of the worst periods of my life. My father was in the Navy, and we were stationed in Hawaii. One day my father came home carrying a little white bundle of fur. She was supposed to be the family dog, but we bonded instantly. I named her Tinker Bell after one of my favorite Disney characters.

When Tinker was two-years old, I had been searching for her for several days, but I couldn't find her. Finally, I found her hiding under my parent's bed… sick. We took her to the veterinarian and left her there for him to perform tests. That night the doctor called and told my mother that Tinker was very sick with distemper. He said that nothing could be done and asked permission to put her to sleep. He said that she would not make it through the night. My mom let me make the decision, since Tinker was my dog. I told her no, because I was going to pray for her. My mother told the vet my decision, and again he emphasized that she wasn't going to live through the night.

I went to my bedroom and through my tears I asked God to heal my little dog. With the faith of a child, I knew that God could heal her. It never entered my mind that He might not heal her. The next morning the telephone rang early. It was the vet and he could hardly speak. "Mrs. Zachary, I came into the clinic this morning fully expecting to find Tinker dead, but instead I found her running around her cage! I cannot explain it, but Tinker is fine, and you can come pick her up. We have no medical explanation for what has happened." My mother explained that I had prayed for God to heal Tinker. He said, "Well, I wasn't a believer before, but I am now! There is no medical explanation for what I witnessed." That God would care about a little girl and her little dog made a profound impression on my life, and on the doctor as well!

It was then that I began to realize that I wasn't just a speck on the earth. Our Almighty God was watching me and heard my prayers, and He loved me so much that He answered my prayer. It may not seem like much, but to me it was everything. I realized that I was important to God!

As I became older, I saw the power of praying to the God of all gods. My tears and prayers were not insignificant to Him. I mattered so much to God, that He sent His Only Son to die for me, that I might have eternal life with Him. What an awesome God we have! Throughout my life I have recalled that event with Tinker many times. God took a little dog and healed her to show me His grace, mercy and undying love.

2

HEART TO HEART WITH GOD

During my studies to become a forensic shrink, I had specialized in Criminal Profiling and Hostage Negotiation. This was what I really loved. I enjoyed and had a knack for deciphering human behavior. It is a two-edged sword when you learn to study people. I can tell when someone is lying to me, and it is awkward knowing that a friend or loved one has just told a lie. You can either pretend it didn't happen, or confront them with the truth and alienate them. I found out that it was best to just keep my mouth shut.

It was during this time that I made a career change. I felt led by God to work with our military's warriors that were coming back physically and emotionally wounded. I was to work with those coming back with PTSD, the hidden wound that really damages the warrior and his family. Being from generations of military men, my loyalty has always been with our troops.

I enjoyed being able to talk to the men one-on-one. They needed someone who understood them and who would just listen and offer advice as necessary. Most of them had physical wounds, but it was the wound in their hearts and minds that were so devastating. "God, You led me to do this, and now I need Your Holy Spirit to guide me and give me wisdom in talking with my troops. Father, I ask for their healing in Jesus' Name."

I was walking into the Federal Building in Little Rock, Arkansas, to get document for a patient, when I slipped and fell and did a split in front of all the federal officers! They came running to help me up. They were all asking, "Are you okay?" I asked them to just help me to my feet, and I would be fine. As they pulled me up, my right knee buckled, and I could not stand. I knew I was in big trouble. I had blown out the knee that I had been trying for years to protect! One officer made the decision to call 911. I was humiliated, lying on the sidewalk in downtown Little Rock with a swarm of federal officers around me.

The ambulance arrived, and I was taken to the hospital. By now the pain was so excruciating that humiliation was the least of my worries. At the hospital, I was taken to get the CT scan of my knee.

Then the doctor came in with the news. "Well, Doctor, you have torn everything in your knee, and you have to have a total knee replacement. I could not believe this. When I was in my twenties, I competed all over the country in Tae Kwon Do tournaments. I was known for my fighting skills and even though I'm only 5'2", I was a force to be reckoned with. I had hurt my knee during this time and had had eight knee surgeries. Yet I kept competing and winning. I was stubborn and wasn't about to let a knee end my tournament days. I was told at the time that I needed a knee replacement and my answer was, "Not in this lifetime!" So, I continued to compete and eventually won the World Championships. And now, after my less than graceful fall, I had to have my knee replaced? So, after 30 years of putting up with knee pain, I had totally blown out my knee. Thank goodness for the pain meds they were giving me.

As I lay on the bed in the emergency room in the blissful fog of pain medicine, my thoughts went back to almost thirty years before. During my Tae Kwon Do days, I had also begun to compete in the Miss America Pageant System. For my talent, I played classical piano. I was preparing to compete in the Miss Johnson County Pageant in Arkansas, when I had to go in for knee surgery again. But, this time there was a problem, and I had to have several surgeries. I was released from the hospital the day before the pageant festivities began. Even though I was favored to win, everyone was skeptical when I said that I was still going to compete.

In Arkansas, the Miss Johnson County Pageant is the prestigious start to the Johnson County Peach Festival. There were many events that I was required to attend, including a parade and a street dance. It's no wonder my mom always called me stubborn. If I make up my mind that I'm going to do something, then I'm going to do it!

I was sitting on the back of a float in a parade wearing an evening gown. The June temperature in Arkansas was scorching, I had just had knee surgery and now I am roasting to death. Sweat was literally pouring off of me, when out of the crowd an angel in the form of a strange woman ran out to me and gave me an ice-cold Coke. I never knew who she was, but I've never forgotten that small act of kindness.

So, not only did I have a freshly operated on knee, complete with a row of staples, but I was out of practice on the piano but I was determined to compete in the pageant. Looking back at all of that, all I can think is "How in the world did I do that?!"

The question that all my advisors had was, "How are you going to manage the swimsuit competition?" Okay, I've gone this far. There has got to be something I can do! Well, call me innovative, but to the amusement and the extreme horror of most people, I had the local county mortician show up at the pageant and he applied makeup normally reserved for corpses, on my knee! I competed in the Miss Johnson County Pageant, and came in as first runner-up! I did go back and compete the next year, win the title and go on to compete in the Miss Arkansas Pageant, but needless to say, I impressed a few people with my tenacity! My mother just shook her head. If you want me to do something, just tell me I can't!

In January of 2011, I had my knee replaced, and it was the worst pain I had ever gone through, including giving birth to three children. When I was finally discharged and went back to my apartment, I was feeling sorry for myself. I was getting out once a day to go to physical therapy, and that was it. The pain was horrendous, and it was a definite low point in my life. I had just bought a Bichon Frise puppy in December, so on February 14, 2011, little Miss Mia Valentine came to live with me. Having a puppy to take care of was a challenge, but at least I had someone to talk to.

One day I laid on the sofa thinking about my life. I had been married, had children, gotten divorced, had all the education a sane person could possibly endure. I was where I wanted to be career wise, but I was lonely, and I wanted to get married and have a real husband this time—a Christian husband, one whom I could love and respect.

James 4:2 says that we have not because we don't ask. *"Okay, God… Let's talk."* I laid on my sofa and just talked to God. I reminded Him of the previous verse in the Bible. *"You said I don't have, because I haven't asked you, so I'm going to hold You to Your Word. I want a husband!"* I was tired of being in charge. I wanted a husband who would make the decisions—one whom I could obey. Did I really just say that? Okay, a husband I will try with God's help to obey!

And then I proceeded to lay out my "laundry list" of what I wanted in a husband. *"Most importantly, he has to be a Christian. I want someone who shares my love of all things forensic."* Most people get a little weird when they see my books on serial killers, psychopaths and sociopaths! *"He has to have a great sense of humor, and he has to be intelligent. I want someone I can talk to on my level. I want a patriotic man, who loves God, Family and Country. And he has to love dogs! He must love music, preferably Classic Rock and Southern Gospel. It would be nice if he* was *handsome, but that is not a priority. I want someone who really gets me. And, lastly God, I want him to be military or retired military."* Being a Navy Brat, I was comfortable with military people. And then, like Sarah in Genesis 18:12, I laughed at God and said, *"Good luck with that!"* Remember, I was getting out once a day to go to physical therapy. How in the world was I going to meet Mr. Right like that?

I learned an important lesson from that conversation with God. Never, *ever* laugh at God or doubt Him! One week after that heart-to-heart with God, I got a call from a supervisor where I worked with Wounded Warriors. "Hey, Kelly! I just remembered something. There was this officer I knew from the Navy, and I think the two of you would really have a lot in common. Here is his email address, why don't you send him a note?" I didn't really have anything to lose, but Dr. Ron Arnold lived in North Carolina, and I lived in Little Rock—not exactly on the short list for a husband, but I sent him a message, and he was right.

We had so much in common that it was scary. We emailed for about ten days, and then agreed that he would call me. Our first phone call lasted seven hours! When I got off the phone, I knew I was going to marry this man. I looked toward the heavens and got humble very quick. All I could say was, *"Wow! You're really fast!"* Ron had also hung up the phone knowing that he was going to marry me. When it's from God, you just know when it's right.

From then on, we talked for six or seven hours every day. Ron had a I.T. firm and was going to Texas to open a branch. When he told me this he said, "I'm stopping in Little Rock to pick you up, and we're going to get married." He picked me up, and after a month and a half of knowing each other, we got married! We fell in love with each other without ever having seen each other. That was six years ago, and we have never once regretted our decision. He is my best friend and my soul mate, and a great gift from God! We both had degrees in criminal justice, and while I went the route of forensic medicine, he took the route of forensic I.T. Isn't God awesome? And, for the record, he is stunningly handsome! God gave me a bonus. I gained a husband whom I adore, Mia gained a daddy, and we were moving to Texas, the birth state of my Marine grandfather, Papa.

3

TEXAS

Ron came to Little Rock in June of 2011, loaded up all the important things I wanted to take with us, and the three of us headed to College Station, Texas, to stay with a Navy buddy of his until we got married and got our own place. On June 20, 2011, I became Mrs. Ron Arnold, and Mia became Mimi Arnold. Ron gave her that nickname, not knowing it was what my children had called my mother. Mimi fell in love with Ron and became Daddy's little girl.

When we look back, it all sounds so crazy! Our first phone call was on May 7th, and we got married on June 20th! I took God at His Word, and He gave me the best husband in the world. I had never been so happy. Looking back at it now, I didn't really know what an incredible husband He had given me. It would be through a test of fire that Ron would prove himself to be a husband above all husbands. I was still having the tachycardia, especially at night. I was also tired a lot, and slept a lot. I knew it wasn't depression, but what was wrong with my heart?

While in the Navy, Ron had made a name for himself in computer technology. He had spent a lot of his time stationed aboard the USS Kennedy. She is an aircraft carrier, and Ron traveled the world aboard her. He had even been aboard the aircraft carrier USS Kitty Hawk, which had been my father's ship, and I had practically grown up crawling on her decks. When he retired from the Navy, he worked in the corporate world as well. He retired from that to open his own I.T. firm.

While we were in Texas, I told my primary care doctor of the heart issues I was having, but since the tachycardia happened mainly at night, it was difficult for him to see what I was explaining, so he sent me to a cardiologist, and I tried to tell that I was having heart problems. When I would get on a bike in the gym, the cardiac monitor showed that within a minute my heart rate would jump to 160 beats a minute. This wasn't good. I told the doctor, and he told me the bike was broken. I told him that I had tried all the machines in the gym with the same result. "Dr. Zachary-Arnold, your heart rate is not jumping to 160 beats a minute!" Ron argued that he was standing right there with me and saw it, but the arrogant doctor wasn't buying it. I turned around and stormed out of his office.

Every time I went to the doctor, my resting heart rate was between 100 and 120. Am I the only one seeing a problem here? I refused to go back to that cardiologist. I decided to just ride things out for a while. But, then one day I went to bed that night and didn't wake until five o'clock the next evening. Something was wrong, but no one would listen to me.

I continued on, just keeping an eye on my symptoms. I was tired, I had tachycardia mainly at night, and I slept a lot. I didn't really do much. I was still able to get up and cook for Ron, and he put on some weight that he had really needed. Life for us was quiet, but good. We had each other, and that was all that mattered. We didn't really want to get out in the Texas heat, anyway, so our life revolved our home.

One night I had gone to bed before Ron. He was working on a coding project for his company and would be up for a while. When Ron came to bed, he was having trouble getting me to respond. I was incoherent and ice cold! Ron immediately called 911. I have vague memories of the paramedics working on me, but one thing I heard was when one paramedic turned to the other and said, "She only has a blood pressure of 60/30!" That got my attention. The doctor in me knew that a blood pressure that low was barely able to sustain life! I was put on an I.V. and put in what is called a Modified Trendelenburg position which positions my legs thirty degrees higher than my head to allow the blood to flow to vital organs. I was then taken Code 3 to the emergency room.

I was admitted to the hospital and put on a heart monitor. I was kept there for about a week while they monitored my heart and my blood pressure. The only conclusion that the doctors could agree on was that for some reason my blood pressure crashed, and my heart was the next to go. I was put on medications to control the tachycardia and discharged with instructions to follow up with the same cardiologist that had told me that my heart rate was not jumping up to 160 bpm. Well, that wasn't going to happen. He wouldn't listen to me before, and I really didn't have much assurance in him, not to mention I really didn't like his bedside manner!

Then one day, we got a phone call that would change our lives. Parson Corporation had gotten in contact with Ron, stressing that he was needed back in I.T world. We were moving to Shreveport, Louisiana. Ron knew that his job would involve him traveling, so he decided to get me a bodyguard. He bought me a blue, Neapolitan Mastiff puppy! His grandfather was the World Champion and weighed 220 lbs!! When we got Mason, he was eight weeks old and weighed thirty-five pounds! Poor Mimi didn't know what to think. Mason took his job seriously and bonded with me on a serious level. He won't let me out of his sight. When I clean house, he is right at my side. Mimi and Mason became best friends. They are like Mutt and Jeff!

My step-son, Brandon came to visit us before we had to leave for Shreveport. I loved having him with us. I literally had a red-headed step-child! He was an incredible young man with his red hair and freckled handsome face. The only problem was that he had a hollow leg! He was always hungry! Brandon was born with an identical twin brother, Tyler Anthony, who sustained Encephalitis at birth and then died when he and Brandon were ten-years old. Oddly enough, my son is named Anthony Tyler.

I've never seen anyone eat so much in one day. Brandon ate like the offensive front line of a pro football team! I was always cooking to keep him fed, but I loved it. Mimi and Mason loved their "Big Brother." Mimi was always taking a nap on Brandon while he watched T.V. Brandon and I developed a good relationship, and we enjoyed spending time together.

One day Brandon and I were watching a movie, when I got up to go to the kitchen. I took a few steps and passed out. Brandon, who was terrified, yelled for his father. When Ron checked me over, I was barely breathing. Brandon had called 911 and put Ron on the line with the dispatcher. Ron told them that I was barely breathing and that my pulse was weak and thready. The dispatcher had Ron tell her when I would take a breath. "You need to start CPR on her and help her breathe." So, my husband began breathing for me while Brandon went outside to wait for the ambulance to arrive.

When the paramedics arrived, they took over for Ron. I remember fading in and out of consciousness, and my first thought was "What are all these people doing over me?" They were putting me on oxygen, placing a C-Collar around my neck, starting an I.V., repeatedly taking my blood pressure. I felt so out of control. It is quite frightening to have people doing all these invasive procedures to you, and you can't stop them.

I was taken to the emergency room, where it was determined that my blood pressure and heart rate had dropped so low that it couldn't support my respirations. I was given meds to bring up my blood pressure, and once I was stabilized, Ron was able to take me home. Once again, we knew there was a problem, but what was it? *God, what is wrong with me? Please let someone find an answer. Father, I'm scared!"* I was like a child crying out to God for help. I needed my Father to comfort me and take away the fear.

I adore Brandon, and it really touched me when he said that he had never been so scared in his life. He was barefooted, running around outside to signal the paramedics my location. I really hate that I scared him so badly. He's had enough loss in his life, and the last thing he needed was to see his dad performing CPR on his step-mom.

While we were waiting for the "Go" signal indicating all Ron's clearances were done, Ronbo and I were asked to teach at a local college. Ron had agreed to teach Information Technology, and the Director of Education, Dr. Tara Neal, had begged me to teach in their Medical Program. I turned her down thinking that I wouldn't be physically up to the job, but she was very persistent! Finally, I agreed to come in and talk to her about teaching one class. This was on a Friday, and when I left her office, I ended up teaching *two* classes, starting that Monday! This had never been a dream for me, but they were desperate for a professor, so I agreed. To this day, Dr. Tara Neal and I have remained good friends. She is a brilliant woman with a Harvard degree, and I could sit and listen to her for hours.

It had to be God's will for me to teach. While I had to sit down a lot, I was able to do the job, and it felt good to be productive again. My emotional status improved greatly. It has always been on Ron's "bucket list" to teach college, but it never really entered my mind. I liked being in the thick of medicine, but I had a great time being a college professor at the same college as my husband. I loved my students and it wasn't too taxing on me, physically. I enjoyed being a positive role model for my students. So, as Parsons Corporation was getting Ron's clearances, we taught college. Even to this day, we are both still in touch with some of our students.

4
THE MOVE TO SHREVEPORT

The call finally came for us to move to Shreveport. They had gotten all of Ron's clearances done, and they were ready for him. "We need you in Bossier City in a week." Bossier City is just across the river from Shreveport and is where the Command Post is located. I just about lost it when Ron told me that we had a week to get moved! Parsons Corporation was sending a relocation company, but we did not have a place to live. I was in a panic! I found a realtor in that area and told her what I was looking for. When you have a dog who is going to weigh 200-lbs, you need just the right house. I found the perfect house on a Friday afternoon. Our realtor said that the leasing office was closed, but she would call first thing Monday morning.

Monday morning our realtor called. "Kelly, I am so sorry, but I have bad news. The house leased out Friday afternoon." I was devastated. *Okay, God. I'm trying to trust You, but I'm struggling right now. Please help us find the perfect house.* The realtor said she had found another house and was sending me the link. She went over to the house and took pictures of every inch of it. "Kelly, this is the perfect house! It's even better than the last one!" I loved it. God had come through once again. At the time, I didn't realize how much the hand of God would impact us moving into this home.

The move from College Station, Texas, to Shreveport was uneventful. The relocation company had boxed up everything and would move our belongings to our new home. We arrived late one night, but since we both were Navy, and knowing how things work out, we had rented a small U-Haul with our "Go Boxes" and a mattress. The house was huge! It was just what the family of a Neo Mastiff needs. We found our bedroom and brought in the mattress and our Go Boxes. Mimi and Mason didn't know what to think! They had moved from an apartment to a 3,100-square foot home with a backyard. They slept close to our bed that night. We had brought Mason's bed with us, and Mimi always slept with us.

The next morning, we were unpacking the rest of the U-Haul, when our next-door neighbor, Janie Jones peeked in. She was older than us, and very sweet and friendly. The first words out of her mouth were, "Do you have a church to go to yet?" I told her that we were Church of God or Assembly of God but hadn't found a church yet. She said, "So are we! You can go to church with us this Sunday!" Her enthusiasm was infectious, and I told her we'd love to go. She explained that most of the people around us were family and all went to Shreveport Community Church. Wow! Thanking God for His goodness in putting us in just the right house, in the right neighborhood, with just the right neighbors, I couldn't help but think how upset I had been when we didn't get the first house. God always provides, and He knows just what we need, if we will only trust and obey. It is hard for me to "let go and let God." I'm used to being in control of my patients and being the decision maker. I had to learn to relinquish control and realize that God knows the big picture. I just see things at that moment. Time after time, God has always provided, and if I just let Him, He provides so much more than I could have ever dreamed.

Shreveport Community Church was well-loved by the congregation as well as the community.

We were so happy in Shreveport. Janie and Charlie's family adopted us, and we felt like we belonged to a large, loving Christian family! Charlie and I had developed a sweet relationship. Charlie was suffering from a form of Parkinson's Disease and couldn't get around very well. He was one of the sweetest men I had ever met. I would go over just to talk to him. Charlie shared my love of anything sweet, so I was always bringing him some treat. Ron enjoyed talking with Charlie, as well. They both shared a love of fine cars. Charlie had a Porsche parked in his garage, that Ron would have given his right arm to take home!

Next-door to Charlie and Janie Jones was her brother, Dan Tilton, and his beautiful wife, Peggy. We were thrilled to find that Dan and Peggy loved football as much as we did. We ended up riding with them to all of the Shreveport Community Church football games. Their school was named Evangel, and they had a high school, junior varsity and junior high football teams. We would sit next to them in the bleachers, bundled up from the cold air, eating the best fried catfish and fries we had ever had! Many mornings I would go next door to Janie and Charlie's and just walk in the back door. It was an open-door policy. I enjoyed having a cup of coffee with Janie, sitting in their kitchen talking, while Charlie watched T.V. in their den. They were always inviting us over for dinner.

Ron was loving every minute at the Command Center. Most Sundays we rode with Janie and Charlie to church. Ron was a new Christian, and he just blossomed at our new church. As we went into the fall, I was asked if I would take on the job as the football team doctor for Evangel Academy, the church's school. Even though they were *just* a church school, they have been the Louisiana State Champions for eleven years! Oh, yeah! Ron and I are avid football fans, and this was a dream come true. God was blessing us in so many ways. He wasn't just meeting our needs, He was giving us our desires as well. It was at this time that we found out that the pastor had once been a professional football player! No wonder their football team was so awesome!

I loved being on the sidelines of the football game. I was told that it was an easy job and "nothing ever happens!" Yeah, sure. My first game consisted of a concussion, two knee injuries, sprains and pulled hamstrings. During one game, this one awesome player was coming off the field soaking wet and freezing! I went over to evaluate him. I was afraid he was going to dehydrate. When I felt his forehead, he was burning up! The poor kid had the flu but was out there giving it his all. What a guy! Much to the dismay of the coaches, I pulled the kid from the game. I had to take off his jersey and pads and find something dry to put on him. The coaches and I would get into arguments when I would pull a kid out of the game for medical reasons. They definitely didn't believe in "mothering" the boys! One boy I suspected had broken his foot, and the coach wanted me to just put his shoe back on and send him back in! No way! I sent for his mom and told her to take him to the emergency room. The next week the kid was there on crutches, with a broken foot!

I had made Ron my assistant. He got where he knew just what I needed, and would be handing me wraps, tape, or bandages. Ron had as much fun as I did. The only problem I had was when they yelled "Doc" from the middle of the field, and I had to run out there. I couldn't breathe. But I loved what I was doing. I loved my boys, and even though I had to take a shower the minute I got back home to wash off the smell of "Sweaty Football Player," I was in heaven!

On Thanksgiving that year Ron had to work, so I was invited over for the family Thanksgiving next door. There was so much food, and the best part was I didn't have to cook it. When Ron got home, he had several platters of food waiting for him! Life was great, but I was beginning to really have bad heart problems now. If it hadn't been for the love and compassion from our adopted family, we couldn't have made it.

It was about this time that I was admitted to the hospital with a host of problems, that we would find out later was because of my heart. My G.I. system wasn't getting the oxygenated blood it needed to function properly. My colon stopped working and I became severely constipated. One night my stomach had swollen to the point that I looked nine months pregnant. My stomach was as tight as a drum and I couldn't breathe. I was in dire need of help. My stomach was so distended I couldn't sit up, but I couldn't lie down either, because then I couldn't breathe. My diaphragm was being compressed and I could only take small, short breaths that threatened to put me into hyperventilation.

It was humiliating to walk into the E.R, only able to wear a pair of surgical scrubs and to be asked when "I was due." Little did I know that the humiliation had only just begun. I was admitted and was given every available method to relieve constipation, but nothing worked. I was miserable. The doctor began giving me injections into my stomach. I had an I.V. in my arm and of course I was not allowed anything to eat. Nothing else could go into my stomach, there just wasn't any room.

I was in the hospital for a week. Every day Janie would come see me. That really touched me. It isn't easy for her to get out, because Charlie can't get out of his chair without her help. His balance was completely gone. He was falling on a daily basis, and that was with Janie helping him stand. That she would go to the effort of visiting daily proved her love for me.

One day she was there, and she was looking at me with concern in her face. "Kelly, your skin is transparent!" She said she was really worried about me. Daily, I was getting laxatives and enemas, but nothing could get things moving along. Every day, Janie would pray for me. I was so blessed to have her and her family in our life. Her family members would also come to see me, but not as often as Janie did. Finally, things started to move along with a vengeance. I felt like I was living in the bathroom, but at least I could breathe now. Once my colon cleared out, I told the doctor I was going home. I had things to do for Christmas.

When Christmas rolled around, we were so excited! It was our first real, full-blown Christmas. We went out and chopped down a tree and spent days decorating. Peggy Tilton had given us a bunch of fruitcake cookies. I can't stand fruitcake, but after I took one bite, I was hooked! It was the best cookie I had ever eaten. Ron fell in love with them, and when Peggy found out, she kept Ron with a constant supply of cookies. My husband made sure that I got the recipe from her. They really are *that* good!

Janie had two older sisters, Betty and Hilda. Both of them were precious. We all sat together as a clan in church! Betty sang like an angel, and I enjoyed sitting next to her. Their only living brother, Dan, was the man you could call if you had any problem at all. He could do anything! He was an usher at church and had endless energy. His wife, Peggy, not only made those incredible cookies, but she was a fabulous cook. Their home always smelled like a bakery.

When I found out that we were going to host the Christmas party for Ron's office, I panicked a little. I love to cook, but I just wasn't up to doing it, so I had it catered. But then Janie and the Tilton family pitched in to help me set up and decorate. I had always wished that I had come from a large family, and after seeing the Tilton "Kids," I was even more convinced! Our home was large enough for the party, and most of the guys Ron worked with wanted to see Mason the Mastiff! The party was a huge hit, but I was so tired afterward that I slept for two days.

On Christmas morning, I felt like a kid opening presents! And of course, Mimi and Mason had plenty of presents, too. Ron had bought me my dream gift— an electric Grand Piano. I hadn't played the piano in thirty years, but I really wanted to get back into it again. I had been cooking for days, and we spent the day eating and talking about how God just kept blessing us!

My health was getting worse. Most days I just stayed home while Ronbo worked. It gave Ron comfort to know that I had help just next door, if I needed it. We were fortunate to find a wonderful family doctor. I told him about my heart, and he immediately called a cardiologist and ordered a weeklong Holter monitor for me. I was finally getting a doctor to take me seriously, and the health care there was wonderful. We were scheduled to be there two years, so I was confident that they could find out what was wrong with my heart. I was hooked up to the Holter monitor and I prayed that it would show something. Anything.

A few nights later, I woke with my heart pounding out of my chest and I couldn't breathe. Not wanting to wake Ron, I went into the den and laid on the sofa. I just couldn't get comfortable. I sat up, turned over, tossed and turned. My chest hurt, and I couldn't catch my breath. I was glad I had the monitor on and that it would probably show what had happened that night. Several hours later I was finally able to sleep, but it was fitful.

After a week, I turned in the monitor and waited for them to download the results. I went about life as usual. Once again, I didn't hound the doctors. I think deep down I was afraid to find out. Ron and I discussed it, and we had convinced each other that the diagnosis would be nothing bad. I would probably get a pacemaker and would live a normal life. But deep down I was afraid. *"Father, give me the strength and grace to handle whatever comes our way."*

5
THE PHONE CALL

The day had started out like every other day.

Ron had gone to work early that morning and I had slept in. That is, until the dogs decided it was time for me to get up and ganged up on me! Try telling a 200-pound Mastiff that you want to go back to sleep. It doesn't work.

It was a beautiful day in Shreveport, and I was fortunate that I didn't have to walk the dogs. I just opened the French doors leading to the backyard and let them have the freedom to run as they pleased.

Mason was barking as we heard the sounds of our neighbor working in her backyard. It was a day that made you happy to be alive. The flowers were in bloom, birds were flying from tree to tree, and Mason was digging up a flowerbed for the hundredth time. I could see the dirt flying through the air before it landed on the patio. He was never going to outgrow his puppyhood!

I gathered up what I was going to need to camp out on the sofa in the den. Water, cell phone, glasses, T.V. remote and my Bible. I was all settled in when our 18-pound Bichon Frise, Mimi, came in from the backyard. She was fed up with her "little" brother chasing her, so she sought refuge among my blankets.

I had talked with God and thanked Him again for His infinite wisdom in caring for Ron and me. I knew if anything should happen to me, Ron would have a lot of "family" looking out for him.

I felt like we were in heaven, living in that neighborhood. My neighbor, Janie, had already called me, as usual, to check on me and see if I wanted to come over for coffee or if I needed anything. I was tired and not quite up to visiting, but we chatted on the phone for a long time.

After I hung up from Janie, I was thinking about how blessed we were. God had given us a home right in the middle of the "Promised Land." Janie, Charlie and all their vast family had taken a couple of "orphans" and adopted us, nurtured us and loved us.

What more could we ask for? Even though my heart was getting bad, I was convinced that the doctors in this area would be able to diagnose me, and I could get my life back. I felt so fortunate to have found a doctor that took me seriously. All I had to do was tell him one time that my heart wasn't acting right, and he got me the help I needed. I didn't like wearing the Holter monitor for a week, but at this point, I would do anything to find out what was wrong and get it fixed!

I was trying to figure out what would be easy to fix for dinner when the telephone rang. It was the nurse at my cardiologist's office. I had turned in the Holter monitor two days before. "Dr. Zachary-Arnold, we've been trying to get in touch with you. The doctor needs you to come in right away!"

I immediately went into denial mode, "What day do you want me to come in?" In my mind, I was thinking, *"Oh, this can't be good."*

She said, "The doctor wants you to come in now. Right now!"

I have made a career of studying human behavior, and I can read a person's voice almost as well as I can read their facial expressions. From the tone and urgency of her voice, I went from denial mode to panic mode. I wanted my husband. I needed Ron! I grabbed my phone from where I had dropped it in shock. With trembling fingers, I scrolled though the contacts until I saw the face that I loved so passionately. *"Please, God, let him answer the phone!"*

I was shaking as I called my husband, Ron, at work. "Honey, the doctor's office just called, and they want me to come in right away!" I was trying not to panic, but he could hear it in my voice.

"I'm leaving right now to pick you up." I could hear the tension in his voice. The voice that was so dear to me sounded scared. *Please, Ron, don't sound like this! I need you to tell me that everything is going to be fine. You're my rock. You can't be afraid. I depend on you!*

After several years of having heart problems and no diagnosis, it was with mixed feelings I threw on some clothes and waited for "Ronbo." While I waited I was praying, *"Okay, God, we have been praying that someone would be able to find out what was wrong with my heart. Apparently, they have, and to be honest… I'm scared. Give me the strength to face this and give the doctors the wisdom in treating this."*

My husband of only five years arrived to get me. I could tell he was worried, because when he gets like that, he becomes very businesslike. I was looking for my purse, and he snapped, "You don't need your purse, let's just go!" *Okay, Ronbo… let's get this over with.*

Ron drove like I was in labor and ready to deliver any minute! He was trying to reassure me, "This is probably nothing. You just need a pacemaker, and then you will be fine." He kept repeating this. He was trying to reassure himself as much as he was me.

We were ushered back into an exam room, and it wasn't two minutes before the doctor walked in. I could immediately tell from the look on his face that this did not bode well for us, and the hair on the back of my neck stood up. "I got the results of your Holter monitor, and I don't like what I'm seeing on your printout. For one thing, you've had a heart attack."

The bottom dropped out from under me. Wait a minute, this was not what I was expecting to hear. *"No, God, not a heart attack! I've prayed to You about this. It's just a problem with my heart rhythm, remember? I just need a simple pacemaker, and I'll be good as new!"*

The voice of the doctor penetrated the haze of my fear, "I'm scheduling you for a Stress Echocardiogram right away to see what is going on." A Stress Echo is a Stress Test with an Echocardiogram done within seconds of the test.

The nurse came back into our room with the appointment day and time. It was the next day! I was still trying to wrap my head around my heart attack, and now they want to do a Stress Echo tomorrow? I panicked and started telling them that that was too soon, and my day was already scheduled. The doctor said that he had rearranged his schedule to do this tomorrow. Then the *voice of authority* chimed in, "Kel, you *are* going to do this tomorrow." Now I feel like I'm being ganged up on. The doctor, nurse and now my husband had made the decision for me. I was outnumbered, and I didn't like it at all. I had the irrational thought that if I could just turn and run from the room, everything would go back to the way it was before I had walked into the doctor's office.

I had tears running down my face. Ron took me into his arms, and I began to sob. I'd had a heart attack, and the doctor suspected something else. He wasn't saying anything, and I wasn't asking. I just wanted to go home and crawl in bed and cry. We left the doctor's office in a fog. Later on, I thought about the bad night I had recently, with the chest pain and trouble breathing, and I knew that was when I had the heart attack. I should have called 911 that night, but that isn't how I do things. I wait until I don't have any other choice before I seek medical help.

It was later that I realized that, for once in my life, I had not drilled the doctor on what he thought was going on, or what he was looking for. I have always tended to practice "backseat medicine." I walk into a doctor's office, and I give him my diagnosis and then wait for his "second opinion."

On the ride home, we didn't say much. I saw Ron wiping away tears. I had tears streaming down my face. *God, I can't do this! Where are you? I need you. Please help me!*

We walked like zombies into our beautiful home. Mimi and Mason came to greet us, and they could tell something was wrong. I knelt down, and they began to lick away my tears, which made me cry even harder. I went into our bedroom and crawled into bed and sobbed. What just happened? It wasn't supposed to be like this. I was just going to get a pacemaker for an arrhythmia disorder! I don't remember the rest of that day. I just remember thinking that I had not planned for this. *God, this isn't how we discussed this. Remember? I was just having an arrhythmia disorder that could be cured with a pacemaker!*

6

THE STRESS ECHOCARDIOGRAM

I had gone over to see Janie early the next morning and told her the news. I hadn't felt like talking to anyone the night before. I just wanted to keep my head buried and feel sorry for myself. Ron wasn't any better off than I was, and he had to get up early to go to work. We were both somber and frightened and didn't want the other to know it, but we did.

I stuck my head in Janie and Charlie's back door, "Anyone home? It's me." Janie came from the den, and I stuck my head in to tell my favorite guy hello. Janie was heading to put on a fresh pot of coffee, when I had to turn her down. Janie makes the best coffee ever and it was with much regret that I had to tell her that I couldn't have anything to eat or drink.

"What's up with that?"

I began to sob, and Janie came and took me in her arms and let me cry. When I was finally able to talk, we went into the den so that Charlie could hear. "The doctor called yesterday, and Ron and I had to go into his office. He said that I've had a heart attack and there is something on the monitor that is bothering him, but he didn't say what it was. I've got to go in today and have a Stress Echocardiogram. That's why I can't eat or drink anything, because they are afraid I'll throw up during the stress test."

Charlie has the ability to show such love and compassion with just the look on his face. "You're going to be just fine." It's funny how much we had come to love Janie and Charlie and their family in such a short period of time.

I began to cry again, and Janie just put her arms around me and said, "I'd offer to go with you, but I don't have anyone to watch Charlie." I told her that I really appreciated the offer, but I would be fine. "Be sure and come back when it's over, and I'll have lunch for you." Wow, you can't ask for better family than that.

"Can I have some coffee when I get back?"

Janie laughed, knowing how much Ron and I both liked her coffee. "I'll fix a fresh pot when you get here!"

The day was beautiful. The sun was shining, children playing, birds chirping, but I was mad at everything. It's easier for me to be mad than to be scared. I couldn't eat anything in case I vomited during the stress test and that wasn't exactly encouraging me. I had told Ron that I could do this alone. He really had to get back to work, and it wasn't like he could hold my hand. I arrived at the doctor's office, shaking. *"God, help me do this. I'm scared. I'm really scared! I need You."* I sat in the waiting room, praying. I sounded like a frightened child crying out to her daddy for help.

As I sat there, I thought of all the patients I had comforted through the years. Fear may not be rational at times, but it is real. I thought of the patients I had held in my arms and had even prayed for. I thought of those whose diagnosis was a death sentence, but they didn't know it yet. I remember the sympathy I would have for them knowing that in just a few short moments their world would be knocked from under them. I thought of the elderly woman in pre-op who was about to have both of her breasts removed due to cancer. Instead of being sad, she was comforting those around her. Then she began to sing the gospel hymns she had sung all her life. The entire pre-op room quieted as we all listened and were blessed by her.

I remembered a tragic case that had tested my faith. The parents of a three-year old blond angel had found her having a seizure and then she stopped breathing. The uncle, a paramedic, happened to be there and was able to start CPR on her. She arrived at the hospital and testing showed her to be brain-dead. The parents, in the final act of kindness agreed to have her organs used for transplant. As the mother sat there, holding her daughter for the last few minutes of her life, I asked the mother if she would like me to cut a lock from her beautiful, blond curls. That small act gave them something to hold on to. So many patients, so many stories.

"Dr. Zachary-Arnold, would you come with me?" I was startled back into reality. The nurse stood in the doorway and held the door for me.

My mouth was dry, and I was having trouble speaking. "Just call me Kelly."

We went into the Stress Test Lab, and I changed into a hospital gown. I looked down at myself and had to laugh; a hospital gown and hot pink Skechers is not a good look! It was then that I noticed that our overgrown Mastiff had chewed off part of the sole of my shoe. These were my favorite shoes!

There were several techs in with me, and as they got the equipment ready, one explained the process. "You will get on the treadmill, and we will do the Stress Test, and then immediately you will get on the table on your left side, and we will do the Echocardiogram." Then the humiliating part, "We've put a basin on the table next to the treadmill. If you have to throw up, aim for that."

Okay, great. "I've got to be honest with you, when I throw up, it just follows gravity. I haven't had much practice at aiming!" Fortunately, they were a great bunch and saw the humor in my feeble attempt at joking.

I had to straddle the treadmill, and when it started I would jump on it. That didn't sound too bad. The treadmill started, and I began to have serious doubts. This was too fast! I managed to jump on while holding on to the bars and I began to jog.

"Okay, Kelly, we're going to speed it up now."

What?! I'm struggling as it is! As the tech increased the speed, within two minutes I couldn't breathe, and I had to do this for fifteen minutes. I was huffing and puffing, but then I began gasping for breath. My chest felt like it was on fire and I felt like I was going to pass out. After about four minutes, the tech knew I couldn't go another step and told me to get on the table. They proceeded to do the Echo while I continued to gasp for breath. I was pale and sweaty, and my skin felt cold as ice. I felt like I was trying to breathe with an elephant sitting on my chest. This was not what I had expected. I didn't think it was going to be this hard, and I was not "running the race" very well.

I was really nauseous, and I was upset that I hadn't been able to finish the Stress Test. Maybe they wouldn't be able to get a diagnosis. *Maybe this had all been for nothing.* The thought of that put me in a panic. Finally, they were through and told me to get dressed. Someone brought me a Coke to drink and waited with me until they were sure I wasn't going to pass out. "Doctor, you can leave now. We'll be in touch with you." *Kelly. Just call me Kelly. I don't really feel like a doctor at the moment.*

On shaky feet, I went out to my car and just sat there for a while. I started to pray, *"Okay, God. Good or bad, at least we will know something. Just please give me the strength to handle whatever comes at me."* Then I began to pray for my beloved husband. *"God, please make Yourself real to Ron through all of this. He is a young Christian, and he is really going to need You. Father, give us the faith to get through this together. I'm struggling to keep my faith, and I can't even imagine how it is for Ron. Father, help me. Help us. God, I need you."*

I went home, tired and scared. I went next-door to Janie's to tell her how it went. "Well, I didn't throw up!" Janie was laughing as she hugged me. She had food on the stove and fixed me a plate. I was starving and scarfed up the food while we talked. Having a Christian "family member" next door had turned out to be a real blessing. Many times, I thanked God for not allowing us to lease that first home. I missed my mother and didn't really have anyone that I could just spill my heart to, but Janie was always there for me. To this day we remain family members, and I miss them so much. I've gone back to Shreveport twice and stayed at their home.

7

OUR PLANS FOR THE FUTURE

When Ronbo and I first got married, we used to dream of the future and what we wanted to do. We both love to travel, so we talked about going back to my home in Hawaii. As a Navy Brat, I call a lot of places home, and Hawaii was one place that I really wanted to share with Ron. I really can't call one place home. That is the down side of being in the military.

I always laugh when someone asks me where I am from. I was born in a small town in the Mojave Desert in California, known only to Marines. Twenty-Nine Palms, or as the Marines fondly call it, "Twenty-Nine Stumps" is home to the largest Marine Base in the world, The Marine Corps Air Ground Combat Center. From there I lived in San Diego and Oxnard, California. I wanted to go back and see my "roots."

After kindergarten, we were transferred to the island of Oahu, Hawaii. This is really the place that I can call home, and it was very important for me to go back and visit. Just seeing pictures of Hawaii makes me homesick, and Ronbo had promised me that we would travel there first. I get so excited telling him about the places that I wanted to take him. I was curious whether the church we attended was still there.

When we had first transferred to Hawaii, I was terrified! I was in the first grade, and as far as I was concerned, we were in a foreign country! Hawaii was as different from southern California as you could get. I would have nightmares about the volcanoes, and everyone looked strange. Now, all I can do is dream about getting back there!

We wanted to get an RV and travel the country. Ron has seen the world, but he has never seen the Grand Canyon, so that was first on his list. I wanted to take Ron to see the Painted Desert and eventually make our way to San Francisco, where Papa, my Marine grandfather is buried in a Veteran's Cemetery.

Neither of us had been up north, and we wanted to go see a Dude Ranch in Wyoming. Ron wanted to get a cabin in the hills of Colorado and spend some time there. We had so many dreams, and we would lie in bed talking about what we were going to do first. We even planned on going out of the country. Ron has a good friend in Holland, and we were both excited about going to visit Nico and his family. When Parsons Corporation called, we knew that eventually they would want Ron on the East coast, where the pulse of our nation is located. We were really excited about this. My family had been stationed at Patuxent River Naval Air Station in Southern Maryland, and with Ron being Navy, he had spent much time in Maryland, Virginia and Washington D.C., so this was like going back home for both of us. Another place I call home!

We couldn't wait for the day when we had orders to return to the East Coast. I wanted to live in an area that had actual seasons! And we couldn't wait for our first White Christmas. We talked and dreamed so much that we had everything planned out already. We were like a couple of kids counting down the days to Christmas.

We talked about how on his days off we would travel around the East coast. We could take a train to D.C and visit all the places of history. We talked about going to Ocean City and staying at the Boardwalk. When I was younger, we would go there every summer when we lived in Maryland. I would ride a bike up and down the Boardwalk each day, lie in the sun and play in the ocean. So, that was going to be one of the first things that we would do.

We planned on going into Pennsylvania and travel into Amish country. We would look for flea markets and indulge our love of antique shops. We wanted to go to Colonial Williamsburg, Virginia, and see how our country looked back in her early years. We both love history, and we planned on visiting as many historical sites as we could and find the old battlefields. We even planned on going to Annapolis, and to the Navy Ship Yard. And we wanted to go see Fleet Week with all the Navy ships. For Christmas, we planned on going to New York, walking the streets and shopping, of course!

Life was going to be exciting and filled with love and fun! We couldn't wait until we got transferred back East. We had both worked hard for our careers, and now it was time to reap the rewards of diligence. Ron was a pilot, but he needed to requalify. I was going to take pilot lessons so that we could fly to some of our destinations.

I still couldn't get over how God kept blessing us. We had a marriage that most people just dream about. We loved spoiling each other. I had never known how much you could love your spouse. Even after six years, we still prefer each other's company, even if we're just reading. We could spend days together without seeing another person and never once get bored. God had blessed me with an incredible husband, and I was about to find out how incredible he really was.

8

THE SECOND TELEPHONE CALL

Ron had the day off, and we were just hanging around the house, wondering how long it would be to get the results of the Stress Echo. My phone rang, and it was the cardiologist's nurse. "Dr. Zachary-Arnold, we need you and your husband to come in right away."

My stomach sank, and I began to shake, "We're on our way now." Ron and I looked at each other without saying a word. What do you say at this point? We had said it all before, and now it was D-Day.

We got in the car and, without realizing it, we had driven to the wrong office and had to go across town again. We didn't say much, but we were both praying. *"God, this doesn't sound good. We need you now more than ever. Please give us strength and courage to handle whatever comes at us."*

Once again, we were ushered back into an exam room. It seemed forever before the doctor and the nurse came into the room. The doctor shook Ron's hand, "Dr. Arnold." He looked at me, and I could see sympathy in his eyes, "Doctor." He took a deep breath and said, "I have the results of your Stress Echo. You definitely had a heart attack, but what I had feared most was confirmed. You are in heart failure."

I shook my head, "I'm sorry. What did you say?" Denial is one of the stages of grief.

He went on to explain that I had Diastolic Dysfunction Stage II Heart Failure. "The lower chambers of your heart, your ventricles, aren't functioning well enough to pump oxygenated blood into your heart and the rest of your body. The chambers contract, but they don't release and blood backs up in your lungs. This can lead to pulmonary congestion which hampers oxygenation of the blood in your lungs, resulting in shortness of breath and even death. You also have Mitral Valve Regurgitation" I knew what it was, but he went on to explain to my husband that the Mitral Valve is one of four valves in the heart. The Mitral Valve, which lies between the left ventricle and the left atrium, is composed of a flap that opens to allow blood to flow from the atrium to the ventricle. The flap is supposed to close off to keep blood from flowing backward, but in this case with each heartbeat, some blood from the ventricle flows backward into the atrium instead of moving forward into the aorta. *"God, what is happening? This is not what I had planned!"*

Ron was white as a sheet, and that scared me. Ron is my rock. Ron makes everything better. Ron can fix anything. That he was that pale further stressed me. My rock was scared to death. I had had enough, but the doctor was relentless. "Kelly, you also have Atrial Fibrillation and we don't know why you've had a heart attack."

Seriously? Are you kidding me? Is there anything that isn't wrong with my heart? Suddenly, the face of the arrogant doctor in Texas swam in front my eyes, as I recalled his words to me. "Dr. Zachary-Arnold, your heart rate is *not* jumping to 160 beats per minute. The bicycle is broken." Red-hot anger raised its ugly head, and I wanted to call him and scream at him, "I told you something was wrong, and you wouldn't take the time to listen to me, and now I'm going to die!"

The room began to spin. Tears filled my eyes and Ron was squeezing my hand so tightly as if he could hold on to me to keep me from dying. I tried to remove myself from the situation and go into "doctor mode." As calmly as I could, I asked, "So, how do we fix this?"

The doctor went on to explain that I would be put on different medications. "I want you taking Metoprolol, Ranexa, a Nitroglycerin Patch, Lasix, and sublingual Nitro pills for you to put under your tongue if you're having a bad episode. But, Kelly… there is no cure for this."

I tried to argue with him, "There has got to be a way to fix this!"

He explained that when I reached Stage IV, I would be put on the heart recipient list, because I would have less than a year to live. "Kelly, I'm sorry. I was hoping it wasn't this. You are too young to have this, and I was hoping I was wrong. I'm sorry."

The rest is just a blur. I looked at Ron, my beloved husband and saw the tears coursing down his cheeks. *I'm asleep. This is just a nightmare, and I'll wake up soon.* It was a nightmare, but I was awake, and I was going to die.

The doctor went over the list of my cardiac drugs and how I was supposed to take them. He told me of all the life style changes I had to make. No salt, no caffeine. I couldn't do anything that would tire me, so I had to get plenty of rest. He had saved the worst for last. "Kelly, whatever you do, you cannot let your heart start beating too fast. That will send you into Flash Pulmonary Edema, and it could kill you instantly." He explained that with Pulmonary Edema, I would start coughing and feeling like I'm drowning. My breathing would be labored and noisy.

Weakly, I stood up and held on to my husband. "I can't take anymore. Please take me home. Now!"

Ron drove to the pharmacy to get my meds filled. I just sat in the car in shock. The doctor had told me of one thing I could try: cardio exercise to try and strengthen the heart muscle. It was a long shot, but at least we felt like we were doing something, instead of just sitting around and waiting for me to die.

We let our pastor know what was going on. The Church put me on their prayer list, and I received a great outpouring of love and prayers. The family of God had come through again for us. It gave us peace to know that we weren't alone. Even with all of this, there were times that I would just suddenly break down and sob, "I can't do this! Why is this happening to me? It isn't fair!" The devastation and pain I felt was on a visceral level. It was actual pain. I was going to die, unless a miracle took place. The average life span of someone in Stage I was five years, and I was already in Stage II. "God, how much longer do I have to live?" Sometimes I would wake Ron, screaming in my sleep. I was having a hard time adjusting to this.

Ron went out and bought me a cardio bike that kept track of my heart rate. At first, I could use it for about two minutes before I was struggling to breathe. I would ride as long as I could and then lie down. Then, I'd start over again. I was so depressed. What was the point if I could only do it for a couple of minutes? Taking the Metoprolol was making me really tired. I'd get out of bed and go lie down on the sofa. My cousin, Jan, told me that she had been on Metoprolol and it had made her so tired that she had to stop taking it. I was determined to get my body accustomed to it, but I was sleeping all the time and couldn't do anything. Even taking a shower would wear me out. After a couple of weeks, my body adjusted to the meds, and the pervasive fatigue was better. Now, it was just the normal fatigue associated with the heart failure. I was given detailed information on Diastolic Dysfunction, on what I could expect and a list of things I could do or not do.

I had four vices in my life: Coke, milk, salt and chocolate. When I had first started with the heart symptoms, my husband put me on house arrest and wouldn't let me drink Coke. He bought cases of water for me. I can't stand water, but I put the flavored drops in the bottle and had become quite fond of it. I had to get a salt substitute—which really wasn't that bad—and I got rid of all the real salt. I couldn't risk anything that would make me retain fluid. Each morning, I had to weigh myself. A liter of water weighs 2.2 lbs. I had to keep a close eye on any water weight. I had Lasix to get rid of the excess fluid. Then, I had to start taking potassium to counteract the leg cramps that I got from the fluid loss. The cardiologist told me to drink tonic water, because it has Quinine in it. We got some, and as soon as I felt leg cramps coming on, I would drink a small bottle, and within ten to fifteen minutes, the cramps were gone.

I made an appointment to go back in and talk to the cardiologist now that I had calmed down. I didn't want Ron to know about the appointment. I knew there were going to be things said that he probably didn't need to hear yet. I sat down with the doctor in his office. "Okay, I need to know everything, so I can get myself prepared for it."

He understood what I needed to do. "Kelly, as your heart failure progresses, it will affect the rest of your organs. Of course, your lungs, because of the buildup of blood flow. You will probably begin to experience liver failure, since your liver is not getting enough oxygenated blood. So, you need to keep an eye on that and watch what meds you take and have regular liver function studies done. Your G.I. system may be affected, and you will have a lack of appetite, and you may have trouble with constipation." I had already found out about that… the hard way.

"You will see your heart failing more as time goes by. The symptoms are a weak heartbeat, chronic cough, impaired thinking, fatigue, and of course, shortness of breath."

I felt my chest tightening as we spoke, but I had to do this. I had to ask this question. "Doc, how will I know if I am in stage IV heart failure?"

He looked long and hard at me, "Kelly, when you start having pulmonary edema, you will be in stage IV. Your lungs will feel wet and soggy and you will have a wet cough. You will not be able to lie on your back without feeling like you are drowning. Your chest will rattle when you breathe." I had to ask the question that plagued me. "At that point, how much longer do I have?" He looked long and hard at me. "You will have less than a year to live at best." I had heard enough. The meds he had put me on would increase the contractility of my heart. It wasn't a cure, just a Band-Aid. I was going to die and I didn't know how much time I had.

When I got in the car to drive home, I prayed with a fervent need to talk to my Father. *"Father God, I don't know what to say. I'm scared for me and for Ron. Lord, You have always been there for me, and I really need to feel Your Holy Spirit now. I know that You will never let me down. You were right there with me in every fire I've gone through. Father, I pray for my husband. Give him strength, give him Your peace that passes all understanding. Draw him nearer to you. Help him to handle whatever comes our way. Father, thank you for the five years we've had together, but it's not enough! I prayed for the perfect husband, and You gave him to me. We want more time together, but, Lord, whatever the case… Thy will be done."*

9

A DEVASTATING BLOW

Ron came home from work in September 2016. He was very quiet, and I knew something had happened, but he obviously didn't want to talk about it. That evening we spent what we called a "No Tech Night." It was something we had come up with some time ago. We put away our cell phones, computers and even the T.V. We used this time to read together or learn new things. We had bought some small LEGO Disney figures, and we were putting those together. We had bought an Origami kit, and we were trying to learn how to do that. For the record, it isn't as easy as it looks! We ended up having "Crumpled Ball" fights! We had more crumpled balls than Origami figures, but we are still working on it!

We had gotten quite a few board games, and we enjoyed playing them with each other. A big bowl of freshly popped, buttered popcorn was standard fare. We would usually make a plate of sandwiches that we could eat one-handedly. When the weather was cool, we would start a fire in the fireplace. Those were moments that we still treasure. And we would talk about everything. I loved our "No Tech" nights.

That night we were playing Connect Four, but Ron wasn't playing with his usual level of genius. This game takes concentration and strategy to play both defense and offense, but Ron was losing more than usual. He was making mistakes, which is not like him at all. We finally decided to call it a night. I thought maybe he was just tired. We went to bed as usual and watched T.V. for a while until we got sleepy, and then Ron asked the usual, "Assume the position?" This means I roll over and get my pillows fluffed just right and Ron snuggles to my back. We can sleep most of the night like this. I love it because I'm wrapped in my husband's arms, and I brace my back against him. There was no better way to sleep!

The next morning, I woke with a start! The sun was shining through the window and my husband had slept through his alarm and was late for work. I shook his shoulder, "Honey, get up! You slept through your alarm!" He yawned and stretched and told me that he had the day off. That is always good news to me. I love his days off.

Ron fixed us breakfast, and after we finished eating, he said he needed to talk to me. "Honey, my job here is finished. We are being transferred to Aberdeen Proving Grounds, Maryland in two weeks." I was stunned into silence. We both sat staring at each other.

"Wait a minute! You were supposed to be here two years, not eleven months!" I hadn't even finished unpacking and now we were moving again?

"Well, apparently I worked myself out of a job." Ron had been sent here to get the Information Technology Center up and going. And, as usual, Ron had done his job better and faster than anyone expected, so now they wanted us on the East coast.

I was absolutely floored. Our perfect life here was going to be uprooted. What about our church and our neighbors—our adopted family? What about my doctors? This could not be happening to us. *"Not now, please God. Not now!"* I was crying as if my heart was broken.

Ron pulled me onto his lap. "Honey, we knew what we were signing on for. I am needed in Aberdeen." What could I say? God, Family, and Country. Ron was trying to get me to calm down before my heart rate elevated. "It is what it is. I'm sorry, baby. I know how much you love it here. So, do I. I don't want to leave any more than you do."

I was stunned; all I could do was sit and stare at Ron. If this was a joke, it wasn't the least bit funny, but I knew that no one would do that to him. This was real. We were having to move from our little slice of heaven, and I wasn't happy. I had to gather up medical records for both of us. I had to make sure that I had enough medicine to cover me until we could find another doctor. I had just found one that I liked and respected, and now we have to move. I wanted to crawl back in bed and put my head under the covers, but we had too much to do.

Here we go again. At least this time we have two weeks before we have to drive across the country with a huge Mastiff in the backseat, not to mention poor little Mimi. And I had to find another house… again. This time I had learned my lesson. I was putting God in charge of finding the house. I was getting tired of this. To top off things, we weren't having a moving company move us. It was all up to us… or should I say Ron? I wasn't physically able to do much.

The first thing I did was go next-door and tell Janie. That was harder than telling her about my heart failure. When I told Charlie, he began to cry. Then we were all crying. They had become our family, and we didn't want to leave them.

Growing up as a Navy Brat meant that I never grew up around any family. They were in California and Arkansas, and we were never near enough to visit them. My grandparents would come to visit occasionally, but I never knew my aunts, uncles or cousins. I hate to admit this, but I don't even know the names of my father's siblings. I had one favorite, Uncle Bob, who was also stationed in the Navy, but we lost contact. Except for a few cousins in Arkansas on my father's side, I don't know anyone. I had always wanted a large family and envied those who had one. I had cherished the time in Shreveport with our adopted family, but the time had come to move on.

Ron went to get boxes, while I looked for a realtor in the area. I was blessed to find a realtor in Aberdeen who listened to what I absolutely needed in a house. If God was going to find this house, then I was going to be specific in what I wanted.

Thanks to the internet, I was able to begin searching for homes in Maryland. I found only one that met my specifications, but I was very uneasy about it. The house was out in the country, and there were no other houses around. *"God, are you trying to tell me something?"* I called the realtor about the house and asked if he could go take pictures of it for me, but I could not shake the uneasy feeling I had about that house.

He paused hesitantly, "Kelly, I wasn't going to bring this up, but I have a home listed that has everything you want, and it's only three years old." Since I still had that uneasy feeling about the other house, I asked him if he would take pictures of it and email them to me. "Kelly, there is one thing I need to tell you. The house is quite a bit larger than what you were looking for, but it is in your price range." I told him that wouldn't be a problem and asked him to describe the home for me. "It's a three-story Georgian style home with 4,300 square feet, but that includes a fully finished 1,100 square foot basement with a 110-inch projection screen T.V. at one end and a fully functional bar at the other end." I nearly choked, and I couldn't wait to see the pictures. He was heading out there right away. *"God, if this is anything like I imagine, You have done it again! Praise the Lord!"*

Thirty minutes later the pictures showed up in my email. "Are you kidding me? This house is absolutely gorgeous! *"God, You did do it again!"* The home had four bedrooms, including a large master suite. two walk-in closets (Oh, yeah!), a loft library, and the laundry room was on the top floor near the bedrooms. That is convenient! On the main living floor, there was a formal living room, formal dining room, a powder room, huge gourmet kitchen, a sunroom breakfast nook off the kitchen, and most importantly, the kitchen overlooked the large den with a fireplace. I could imagine myself cooking while Ron took it easy in the den. Our time together is even more precious now than it had been. Downstairs was a man cave that most men could only dream about! It was beautiful. I was picturing Ron and me watching football on that enormous T.V. screen. I'm a diehard Arkansas Razorback fan, and Ronbo is a diehard Tennessee Vols fan! We have come to compromise, and now we actually like each other's teams, except when they play each other! The bar was really nice, but even though we don't drink, we had a sink, and small fridge and more counter space than most homes have! *"God, you are really cool!"* We could have football and Christmas parties down there. The realtor was right, it was perfect!

A few days later we got some news that lifted our mood considerably. About four years ago, we had met a Marine on social media. As time went by, we had fallen in love with David Dahn and his beautiful wife, Carol. David and Ron were constantly jabbing each other. Since Ron was Navy and David was a Marine, the jokes were plentiful. David called Ron a "Duck", and Ron called David a "Naval Reject." David and Carol were on their way to New Orleans and stopped in Shreveport long enough for us to meet them for breakfast. They knew about my health, and they had been part of our support system. That we got to meet them in person was a special gift for all of us. It's not often you become such good friends through social media, but we were fast friends before we even met in person. They were part of my prayer team, and to this day we remain great friends.

Now, all we had to do was pack up. I did as much as my heart would allow, but Ron was having to do the majority of the work. I felt so guilty. Ron never once complained, which actually made me feel worse. Ron had rented a large furniture truck, and I was going to drive my car with the babies in the backseat. It was *only* an eighteen-and-a-half-hour drive! Piece of cake. Who am I fooling? It was going to be a nightmare! Ron said we were going to take it slow, so I didn't get too fatigued. Little did I know that this was going to be a very eventful trip, and not in a good way.

10

THE DISASTROUS
TRIP TO MARYLAND

After everything was loaded and the floors were swept, we said goodbye to our new family. Hugs and tears were exchanged, and then it was time to leave our beloved home. Ron and I held hands as we prayed for safety on our trip. We gave each other a long hug and kiss, and then we looked each other in the eyes. Words were not necessary. We knew what the other was feeling and thinking. Ron told our kids, Mimi and Mason, to behave for Mommy, and off we were to the East coast.

I didn't feel well, but I wasn't about to tell that to Ronbo. He needed to keep all his attention on his driving. I really didn't like the thought of him driving that huge truck, but what choice did we have? I had made sure his Bluetooth was on, so we could talk without him having to take his eyes off the road.

I thought about the trips we had made in our short marriage. First, Ron had driven from North Carolina to Little Rock to pick up his future wife and puppy. Then we had driven from Little Rock to College Station, Texas. That was a unique trip to say the least. The man I had been talking to for a month and a half and had fallen in love with during that time, had told me that we were getting married, and he was coming to pick up me and Mia. Then we packed up and drove away on the first leg of our life together. We had talked a lot during that trip, and I remember just staring at him and smiling. I couldn't believe that we had done this. I couldn't believe that God had pulled this off! We were so much in love with each other. I didn't know it at the time, but when I looked at him and thought how much I loved this man, it was nothing compared to the love that would blossom and grow between us.

And then our family had grown with the addition of our overgrown Neapolitan Mastiff, Mason, and we ended up driving from Texas to Shreveport. That had been an easy trip compared to what was ahead of us.

I don't remember how many hours we drove that first day, but it wasn't what we had planned. Ron had scheduled us an extra day, just in case. I was driving point, so if I needed to stop, all I had to do was pull over. I had gotten so tired that I was beginning to cross the lanes, Ron called and made a unilateral decision to call it a night. We found a hotel, got the kids and our go bags and went into the hotel room and collapsed. We had to get a room with two double beds so that Mason would have room to move! I was so happy to see a large, comfy bed. I laid down hoping that I would fall asleep right away, so I could wake up and hopefully feel better than how I felt at the moment.

I had been feeling pain in my upper right quadrant of my abdomen for most of the day, but I hadn't said anything to Ron about it. The pain was getting considerably worse and without telling Ron, I grabbed a plastic cup off the sink and went into the bathroom. I just wanted to take a look at my urine, just in case. I peed into the cup, and when I looked at it I let out a scream. Ron came running into the bathroom, and I showed him the cup of my urine. It looked like black coffee! Ron frantically asked, "What in the world is *that?!*" I told him that was my urine. I was shaking so hard I thought I was going to spill it, so Ron took it from me. "Ron, I need to find an Emergency Room." Thank goodness for my Garmin GPS. We looked up a hospital and found the only one in the area. I took the cup with me to show the doctor in case I couldn't produce any more urine.

I don't even know what town we were in, but we found a small, one-horse hospital. Ron checked me in and gave them the insurance information. I was taken into the triage room, where a nurse took vital signs and got a history. She had me urinate again, and it was still black. Then a foreign doctor walked into the Triage Room. He had performed a urinary analysis on it. Basically, just a dipstick. He could barely speak English. "Doctor, you just have a urinary tract infection."

I told him that I was not presenting with any UTI symptoms, but he wouldn't budge on his diagnosis. I don't think he liked having a female doctor question his judgment. I asked him what my white cell count was, and it was normal. "Did I have any RBC in my urine?" This would indicate the presence of blood.

"No, that was normal, too."

I was starting to get angry, "What are you basing your diagnosis on? Did you do a liver function study?" He told me that they couldn't do that and besides, it was just a UTI. I was getting seriously angry. I had normal white blood and red blood cell counts, not even any bacteria. I did *not* have an infection.

I looked at Ron and said, "Let's get out of here!" I was sure that the dark urine was indicative of liver failure, but I certainly wasn't going to point that out to my husband. *I'll worry about that when we get to Maryland.* I was determined that I could make it a couple more days, just long enough to get to our new home.

We got on the road early the next day. We got burgers for lunch, and ate in the car since we couldn't take in our giant dog. As we drove, I began to eat. The first time I swallowed, it felt like there was a razorblade in the food. My esophagus was in major pain, and the food came right back up. I couldn't swallow food and had to spit it out. This was a new symptom and I didn't like the implications of it. I called Ron with the news. "Well, at least drink something so you don't get dehydrated." He was concerned, but at this point what could we do? Every time we stopped, Ron got me several bottles of water.

By the time we stopped for the night, I was in serious condition, but I didn't want to tell Ron how much pain I was in. I became diaphoretic, cold, pale and sweaty. It didn't take a doctor to see that I was in serious pain. "Okay, Kel, get dressed and let's go find another E.R." At this rate, Ron and I were never going to get to Maryland! *"God, I really need Your help. You've gotten us this far, but I don't know how much longer I can go on, and I don't want my husband to know everything. Please keep Your hand on us. Protect us. Guide us. And please give me the strength to do this!"*

We found another hospital that seemed better than the last one. This time the diagnosis was Pancreatitis. I was given meds to treat the upper G.I pain I was having. *Come on! This is ridiculous. When is this going to end?*

The meds helped, but I still couldn't even swallow the smallest bite, and it still felt like a razorblade. It may be Pancreatitis, but there was definitely something else that was very wrong. I still couldn't swallow food. It came right back up. *"Father, how long can I go on like this?"* Every time we stopped to walk the dogs, Ron would take Mason who was very happy to get out of the car. I walked Mimi, trying not to double over in pain in front of Ron.

We were determined to make it to Maryland the next day, before I ended up being admitted in a hospital. I never did tell Ron how bad the pain was. Even a drink of water was hurting me. *"God, what is going on? Please help me! Just help me to get to Maryland."* We were all irritable. And if you have never experienced an irritable Neapolitan Mastiff, count yourself fortunate. He wanted out of the car. It had gotten where he wouldn't get back in the car. I had to go to one of the back doors and pull on his leash, while Ron pushed and lifted his behind into the car.

I felt a renewed sense of hope as we crossed the Maryland state line. Soon we would arrive at our new home. I have never been so anxious for a trip to end. Mason would whine unless I let down his window, and he hung his massive head out and soaked up the breeze. The looks I got from other motorists would have been classic had I not felt like I was dying. I'm pretty sure the drivers behind me didn't appreciate the drool flying back on them!

11

ARRIVAL AT OUR NEW HOME

As soon as we pulled into the driveway, we were impressed once again, with the goodness of God. Our home was beautiful. The neighborhood was great! I felt like I was living on base again, but this time with up-scale homes. The neighbors were either military or government employees. We really felt at home. It even looked like the East Coast with all the Georgian and Colonial style architecture. Just down the road from our neighborhood was an historical house that dated back to 1861. You could really see the British influence in Maryland. Prince George's County, Queen Anne's County, Dorchester County and the dreaded roundabout! The first time I got on one, I felt like I was on a merry-go-round and couldn't get off!

I parked on the street, so Ron could back the truck into the driveway. The pastor of a local church and some of his congregation had volunteered to help Ron unload the truck. I got the dogs and brought them into the house. They were so happy to be out of that car. It's would be a long time before they feel like a road trip! Mason was trying to negotiate walking on hardwood floors, and it was not going well for him. He kept ending up sprawled on the floor with all his paws in different directions! It would have been funny, had we not been so tired and with me in so much in pain.

As soon as I got the dogs in the backyard, I used my Garmin GPS to find a hospital. There was a town about ten minutes away with a hospital. I kissed Ron, who admonished me to be careful, and I drove myself to the hospital. The pastor and his crew were due to arrive any time, and the last thing I wanted was them to see me looking like I did.

The doctor was great. She, also, gave the diagnosis of pancreatitis and said I had something going on with my esophagus. At last, a doctor who is listening to me.

She wanted me to follow up with a G.I. doctor and gave me the name of one she had used. She gave me new meds to control the pain and to coat the esophagus, so I could swallow again. She also did a liver function study and didn't like the results. I was in early stage liver failure. My heart, pancreas, esophagus and liver all had problems. I was running out of healthy organs.

I drove back to our new home hoping that my husband would be too busy to ask too many questions. When I arrived, I was relieved to find that they had unloaded everything! The family of God is always there when you need them. They had also done the neighborly kindness that you find out in the country. They had brought fresh corn and tomatoes and a bouquet of flowers. Their kindness really touched me. I was tired, but I wanted to explore our new home. That is when we discovered we had a problem. Mason couldn't go downstairs, because all his wrinkles went forward and obscured his vision! We put his bed at the foot of the stairs. He would go up a couple of steps, but then back his way down. Great! Our dog couldn't go down the stairs, and we had a three-story home! We were all exhausted, so we made our bed and called it a night. *"Thank You God for getting us here safely. Jesus, I really need your healing touch. My body is starting to fall apart, and I'm scared. I'm trying to put my faith in You. While the doctor in me knows the medical reality of this, the Christian in me knows You can heal me."*

We didn't know that we were standing on the precipice of the fight of our lives. We would find ourselves repeating this verse, Deuteronomy 31:6 NKJV, *"Be strong and of good courage, do not fear nor be afraid of them; for the Lord your God, He is the One who goes with you. He will not leave you nor forsake you."*

I did my best to try to unpack, but I couldn't do much. If I lifted a small box, I became short of breath. Ron had to report for duty as soon as we arrived, but he would come home after a long day of work and do the cooking and cleaning. He even did the unpacking. I had become worthless, and the guilt was eating me alive. Ron didn't sign on for this.

I was not able to eat or even drink much. It still felt like I was swallowing razorblades, and the food came right back up. I tried to hide this from Ron for as long as I could. His job was stressful enough, not to mention that he had to do everything at home.

I was miserable. I couldn't help out, I couldn't eat anything and now I couldn't drink anything! I knew God loved me. I knew I was His child, but I was beginning to wonder if I had done something really bad to have all this pain and illness heaped on me. It was around this time that I was going through my mom's Bible, and I saw a sheet from a legal pad with my name on it. She had taken the time to write out a couple relevant chapters in Job. I had chills going down my arms when I read this. Did Mom somehow know that I was going to have a need to read this? I still wonder what caused her to do that. Had God used my mom six years before, to tell me that He knew what I was going through, and it would be okay? A question I will never have an answer to, until I face Him one day.

It wasn't long before I knew that if I was not admitted to the hospital right away, I was going to die from dehydration. So, I told Ron what had been happening. I had to face the wrath of my husband, and it was not pretty. I had already packed a bag, so we left for the same hospital. In the E.R, the doctor took one look at me and said, "I guess you know that we are admitting you?" *Yeah, I had figured that one out already.* My calcium and potassium levels were dangerously low.

I told Ron to go home. "Honey, there is nothing you can do here. You need to stay rested for work and take care of the dogs. Just do that while I'm here. The doctors will take good care of me." Reluctantly, Ron knew that what I was saying made sense. So, he kissed me and held me tight, and we said goodbye. As much as I loved my husband, I just wanted to be left alone in a dark room with no noise. Keep the sensory stimulation at a minimum.

I was hooked up to an I.V. to get fluids in me. They were keeping me NPO, nothing to eat or drink by mouth, because they knew I was going to have to get scoped to see what was wrong. In my room, I set up my cell phone on my bed. That was my lifeline to Ron. Then I settled back to watch T.V. and let the I.V. do its job. It wasn't what I wanted, but I definitely needed it.

If you've ever been admitted to a hospital, you will know that it is the last place to get rest or peace and quiet. It seemed like every five minutes, a nurse would come in to check my monitor my vital signs. They did keep the light to a minimum, but when the lab would come in to draw blood, they began by turning on the brightest light, and in a loud voice announce, "Dr. Zachary-Arnold, we're here to draw your blood! Can you tell me your name? I started to resort to sarcasm and tell them, "You just called me by name." However, I refrained, knowing that it was standard operating procedure.

I had just gone back to sleep when the respiratory therapy repeated the same thing. "Dr. Zachary-Arnold, I'm from respiratory therapy, and I need to draw your blood gases." The doctor didn't like the way my labs were looking and had ordered blood gases to be drawn on me. I had never had blood gases drawn, but as long as they hurried so I could grab five minutes of sleep before the next assault, I'd go along with it. Like I had a choice.

I was trying to doze while they put the tourniquet on me. "Okay, Doctor, you're going to feel a slight pinch." The next thing I know, I'm letting out a bloodcurdling scream! I know the whole floor heard me and possibly the whole hospital. An ABG or Arterial Blood Gas is drawn from the artery instead of the usual vein. They had struck a nerve, literally, and the scream was long and extremely loud! "Oh, I'm sorry! Let me try another spot." *Another spot?! You have got to be kidding me!* It was a good thing that I was too weak to fight back or she would probably have ended up sprawled on the floor. It's amazing what pain can do to a normally kind person with a high pain threshold. It was so bad that if they had to do it one more time, I would have demanded to be put under anesthesia first!

12

MY BRUSH WITH DEATH

I had finally gotten over the assault on my artery and nerve and had gone to sleep when the door slammed open. It was my nurse who ran over to my bed and was looking at the monitor. I was too tired to ask her any questions. She left the room after a few minutes, but this time she left the door open. It didn't matter anyway, I was so exhausted I could have slept through a parade.

As I tried to sleep, nurses kept coming into my room and asking me to wake up. My normally good humor was gone, and I kept telling them to leave me alone. One nurse kept taking my blood pressure and then she asked me to sit up. I sat up, but my head would roll to the side. They were asking me stupid questions, and I was getting very irritable. *Why couldn't they remember my name? It's not that difficult.* Nobody was telling me what was going on. They just kept annoying me.

Around three in the morning, my room began to fill with doctors, nurses and techs. The bright lights had been turned on, and some doctor was yelling orders at the rest of the staff. "Dr. Zachary-Arnold, your heart and blood pressure are crashing and we need you to fight!" He continued to bark out orders for meds to be given and to check my blood pressure constantly.

I just wanted to go to sleep. I actually felt quite peaceful and I knew if they would leave me alone, I could just drift off. "Kelly! We need you to stay with us! *Kelly!* Come on, honey, keep your eyes open!" My blood pressure had dropped into the danger zone. My room was filled with doctors and medical staff, as they tried to stabilize me. My blood pressure continued to drop. Earlier I remember seeing that it was only 60/31. The thought had entered my mind that that wasn't good. I was literally circling the drain.

The doctor had asked the nurse to get my husband here STAT. I didn't know Ron's cell phone number off hand, but I told them it was on my cell phone. Then, to top off everything, my cell phone wouldn't work! It was plugged into the charger, but it wouldn't turn on. I had been having problems with it, but nothing like this. Nobody could find Ron's cell number! "Do you know any neighbor that could get him?" I didn't know anyone where we lived except for my husband! "Kelly, have you filled out a living will?" Vaguely, I remembered one in Texas, but that wasn't going to help now.

"Nurse, get a crash cart in here! If we don't get her blood pressure up, she is going to code!" Earlier the doctor had ordered a liter of I.V. fluid to be given to me. The nurse stood by my bed, squeezing the bag as she tried to get the fluid into me as quickly as possible. Still, I continued to crash and we couldn't get my husband there! I was terrified. As a doctor, I knew the implications of all this. They had a board in my room to keep track of my vitals and the fluids and meds they were giving me, and I couldn't help but read it.

The doctor ordered another liter of fluid to be squeezed into me, but to no avail.

"We're losing her!"

They ended up giving me four liters of fluid. The normal blood volume for a woman my size is 4.7 liters, so they ended up just about replacing all my blood volume, but I wasn't pulling out.

They had moved the crash cart into my room, and had it beside my bed. The doctor had asked me, "Doctor, *when* you code or flatline, what are your wishes for resuscitation?"

I didn't have a living will; they couldn't get my husband, so with witnesses around, I had to tell them what my wishes were. "If I code, go ahead and try to resuscitate me and keep me on life support to the point where I don't have any brain activity." The doctor got the witnesses to sign the form. I couldn't believe I was having to go through this alone.

For six hours, they had worked on me, giving me meds to increase my blood pressure and squeezing four liters of fluid into my veins. They had put my bed into a position with my legs forty degrees above my heart. Finally, they got my blood pressure stable enough to send me into emergency surgery to get scoped and find out if my esophagus was bleeding and causing the problem.

I was rushed from my room into the surgery area. I had piles of blankets on me, because I was freezing! Those bags of I.V. fluids are cold. I looked like a mummy, since all you could see of me was my face. Even my head had a blanket on it "hoodie" style. The operating room was its normal icy cold. People in scrubs and masks were grabbing my precious blankets off of me, untangling me from all the cords and tubes that had me immobilized. I was moved onto the cold operating table, shaking from head to toe. One nurse took pity on me and got a blanket out of the warmer and covered me with it. Through chattering teeth, I managed to thank her.

"God? Where are You? I need you, Father. I need You! Jesus, I claim the name of Jesus!" The anesthesiologist was a huge man, but over his mask, his eyes looked kind. He was asking me questions rapid-fire. It was a sprint to the finish line to get me under anesthesia, and the speed in which everyone was moving was scaring me. The last thing I remember was telling the anesthesiologist, "Please, don't let me die!"

He was a gruff, but caring Russian doctor. He said, "I not let you die. Now shut up and go to sleep!" Then he winked at me. Okay, he lacked a little on the bedside manner, but he didn't let me die.

I woke in excruciating pain. My esophagus felt like it had been ripped in two, and someone had poured acid down my throat! "What was the problem?" I croaked.

The doctor told me that I had an Esophageal Stricture, where the bottom, or distal end of my esophagus had closed off. "We had to go in and dilate it, but you also have Esophageal Ulcers. It's no wonder you couldn't swallow, and it felt like razorblades." I had had reflux for years that I just didn't treat; now it was coming back to bite me. "You will be on a Proton Pump Inhibitor (PPI) medication the rest of your life, and for the next week you can only have liquids. When you can tolerate a soft diet, we will discharge you."

They were giving me a vile concoction called a "G.I. Cocktail." The first time they gave it to me, I would have thrown up, but my poor esophagus just didn't have the strength. This vile concoction contained Lidocaine, and it soon became my best friend. Once I got past the gagging, the Lidocaine kicked in, and the pain relief was wonderful!

They could not reach my husband at work because they didn't know where he worked! I have never wanted or needed my husband more than this, but I knew from our arrangement, that he wouldn't come by until after work. I spent the day on pain medicine and drinking my favorite vile concoction… and sleeping. The staff felt sorry for me and tried to time it where they would all come in at once, allowing me to gain precious minutes of sleep.

They still had me hooked to monitors and an I.V. I had an oxygen mask on and a patient-controlled analgesia in my arm. I had various bags of fluid going into my I.V., and the ominous crash cart still sat beside my bed. I felt strapped to my bed. I couldn't move or roll over. All I had to do was wait for Ronbo to come by after work, and I was afraid his head was going to explode when he saw his little wife covered and surrounded by medical equipment.

13

HUSBAND ON FIRE

P er our arrangement, Ron came by after work.

He walked in the door of my room and looked shocked at all of the equipment that was hooked up to me, not to mention having a crash cart in there. "Are you okay? What is going on in here?!" How do you tell your husband that you nearly died last night and had emergency surgery? "Honey, I had a little problem last night. My blood pressure crashed, and the doctors thought I was going to code. They had to work on me six hours to get me stabilized enough to go into emergency surgery."

It hurt to talk, but from the look on his face, I needed to give him the abbreviated version quickly. Ron was stunned. "Didn't anyone think that I should have been here with you? Why didn't someone call me? Why didn't *you* call me?" He had apparently missed the point about how I almost died. He ranted for a minute before I could tell him about my cell phone. He picked up my phone and called it a piece of junk, and tossed it on the bed. Then, it hit him, "Wait a minute! What do you *mean* you had emergency surgery?!" I was having trouble talking, so I rang for a nurse.

"Dr. Arnold, your wife became critical last night, and we couldn't get your phone number off her cell. She is okay for now, but we are keeping a close eye on her."

Ron had turned a ghastly shade of white. "What are you doing for her? What meds are you giving her? What about her heart? What are you doing for that? He bellowed, "I WANT TO TALK TO THE DOCTOR IN CHARGE OF MY WIFE!" My husband was on fire. Truth is, he had just been scared to death, and he was using anger as the vehicle in which to cope. I've never seen him that scared and angry at the same time. I said a quick prayer of protection for the doctor, and that God would calm down Ron and alleviate his fear. I know my husband; he had just had a grenade thrown at him, and he was alarmingly scared!

The nurse practically ran out to go get the doctor. Ron paced around the room like a caged tiger. I was dreading the arrival of the doctor. He walked cautiously into the room with a sympathetic look on his face. Apparently, he had been warned about the irate husband. "Dr. Arnold, I understand you have some questions concerning your wife's care." Ron started in on him, demanding to know what was being done to keep his wife alive. The doctor explained that I had crashed last night, and they had a lot of trouble getting my blood pressure to stabilize. He went into detail about what they had done for me and the meds they had given me. "Finally, we were able to get her into emergency surgery and fix her esophagus as much as we could."

Ron was livid, "Why didn't you wait until I got here to take her into surgery? You shouldn't have operated on her with her blood pressure so low! She has heart failure! She could have died in surgery, and I wasn't even here with her!" Ron looked like a trapped, injured animal. His eyes were wide and glazed over. This was not going well. People had begun to gather in the hall to witness the commotion.

The doctor was doing his best to remain calm. "Dr. Arnold, we had to give your wife enough I.V. fluids to practically replace her entire blood volume, but her blood pressure and heart rate would not stabilize. We *had* to get her into surgery to see if her esophagus was bleeding. We had to do it immediately before her heart stopped."

Ron wanted to make sure that I was getting all my heart meds. "Is she getting all of her meds?" He needed to make sure that they were giving me the drugs that kept me alive.

"Dr. Arnold, we cannot give your wife any of her heart meds…"

Ron interrupted with a roar, "What do you mean you *aren't* treating her heart? Are you crazy? What kind of doctor *are* you?! Those meds keep her heart beating and keep her alive!"

Husband on fire. The fear that radiated from my husband was tangible. The doctor was waiting for a break in his ranting to explain to him why they were withholding my cardiac meds. "We have a problem. The meds that your wife is on to treat her heart lowers her blood pressure, and she already has abnormally low blood pressure."

Ron was beyond comprehending what the doctor was explaining. "But she will die without her heart meds!"

The doctor decided it was time for tough love, "*Dr. Arnold!* Your wife almost died last night! Yes, she needs her heart meds, but she will die when her blood pressure crashes! Dr. Arnold, we brought in the crash cart because we expected your wife's heart to stop! We *had* to get her blood pressure back up before she died!"

Ron was shaking from fear and fury. "Once we are sure that her blood pressure is going to remain stable, then we can start giving her some of her heart meds. Your wife is in a bad situation. The drugs she needs for her heart lowers her blood pressure. Her blood pressure was not compatible with sustaining life! I'm sorry. We can treat one or the other, and we had to treat her blood pressure before she died."

Ron had stopped screaming at the doctor. Now, he just looked like a defeated child. It was heart wrenching to see him like that. "Do you have any more questions for me?" Ron mutely shook his head. "If you do, have a nurse call me. We have your wife on a heart monitor and the cardiologist is carrying it around with him. If something starts to happen, he'll know it right away."

Ron sat down, and tears began to fill his eyes. "Dr. Arnold, I'm sorry about your wife's condition. This is about as bad as it can get, but we had to do what we knew was in the best interest for her. I *am* really sorry."

I tried to reassure him that I was alright, but all he could say was, "I wasn't even here with you."

I explained that it wasn't his fault, and God had been there for both of us. "Honey, it's okay. I'm fine now." I don't think he even heard me.

My poor husband just sat with his head in his hands and tears coursing down his cheeks. *"Jesus. Jesus. Jesus."* There is power in the name of Jesus, and Ron needed to experience that power.

During that week in the hospital, the doctors took advantage of having me at their mercy, so they did every cardiac test known to man, except for the Stress Test. We all knew I wouldn't make it through that one.

And once again, I had the now familiar Echocardiogram. I didn't ask about the results. I knew I wasn't going to hear any good news, so why ask? At this point, I had given up and stopped trying to be the doctor and just laid in the hospital bed, licking my wounds. *"God, are you there? I don't feel You. I just feel fear. God, do You hear me?"*

Blessed is the man that trusteth in the Lord, and whose hope the Lord is. For he shall be as a tree planted by the waters, and that spreadeth out her roots by the river, and shall not see when heat cometh, but her leaf shall be green; and shall not be careful in the year of drought, neither shall cease from yielding fruit. Jeremiah 17:7-8 KJV

14

I'VE GOT TO GET OUT OF HERE!

I was bored. I had begun to watch Judge Judy and sitcoms on T.V. What you have to understand is that I *hate* reality shows *and* sitcoms, but I didn't have much of a selection from which to choose. I like real reality shows like the forensic shows and medical shows—nothing contrived. I like documentary and history shows. If I watch a reality show or a sitcom, I feel my I.Q. drain from my body. I couldn't read, because I just didn't have the strength to hold up a book.

After more than a week in the hospital, I couldn't take it another day. I was still on liquids, but I could do this at home, and that's where I really wanted to be: home, with my husband and Mimi and Mason.

Besides, they had scheduled me for a colonoscopy the next day, so I needed to make a jail break. Without telling my husband, I checked myself out of the hospital AMA, "Against Medical Advice." I feel it is important for me to bring up this fact; I never lied to my husband, but I did withhold information from him. Ron had enough on his plate with work and having to go home and take care of Mimi and Mason. Trust me, you don't want to leave a 200-pound Neo Mastiff on his own for very long. He had already eaten the sofa pillows and eight television remotes. I don't condone what I did, but at the time I thought it was in Ron's best interest.

It felt good to walk back into the home that I barely knew. Most of our move to Maryland consisted of me being in the hospital, and the woman in me needed to make a home for my family. I am OCD when it comes to my kitchen. The first things that I have to get done are to organize the pantry and the spice cabinet. As things turned out, it took me until after April before I was able to accomplish this task. Ron once made the comment, "I knew you felt really bad when you didn't organize the pantry!" I always have the cans separated into veggies, fruit, soup and all the labels face forward. It might seem a little OCD, but to me it is just convenient!

I had a large kitchen, but I didn't like where everything was stored, and that was driving me nuts, but I just didn't have the strength to go and rearrange everything. I tried not to go into my closet, because I just got depressed! Everything was hung up, but it wasn't organized like I've always done it. I have the dresses, tops, pants, skirts separated into seasons and colors. My sweaters are folded and sorted into styles and colors and are in the top of my closet. Now my closet looked like a garage sale gone bad! I certainly couldn't ask Ron to do that for me. He would have *no* idea what I needed him to do. So, when I walked into the closet, I just grabbed something and got out of there!

But, for the time being, it was going to have to work. I would walk around and try to do a little at a time, but as soon as I did, I would turn pale and clammy and my heart output was compromised. *"God, help me to be grateful for this beautiful house and not stress that it isn't arranged like I want it. Thank you for Ron, and that he took it upon himself to do this for me!"*

Feeling the need for some sunlight, I went out in the front yard. A neighbor came over and introduced herself to me. Her name was Lisa Gordon, and she lived two houses away from me. She invited me to a cooking and baking ware party the next night. "A lot of the neighbors will be there and it will be a good way for you to meet everyone!" I liked Lisa right off the bat. I didn't tell her of my medical problems, but I did agree to come to the party. I so badly wanted to feel normal and do things that normal people did. She was telling me who lived where, and what their husbands did. She pointed out who did the big Halloween House and how everyone really got into decorating for Christmas. I liked Lisa right away and was relieved when Ron didn't come outside and turn down the invitation with a detailed explanation of my heart problems.

Ron was more than a little skeptical when I told him I had agreed to go to the party. Honey, you just got out of the hospital after almost dying and having emergency surgery!" *Yes, Ron. I was there, and I know what happened.* He knew that I wanted to feel normal again, so taking pity on me, and with many admonishments from him, I went to the party. Ronbo told me if I began to feel bad to call him, and he would come get me. Yeah, that's not going to happen. I didn't want to stand out from the rest of the wives.

I got dressed early, so that I could lie down and rest before I had to go. Ron was still staring at me intently, like he expected me to keel over at any minute. "Honey, I'll be fine. I won't stay very long. I promise." My husband stood in the front yard while I walked across the street to Lisa's house. My thoughts jumped back to when we lived in Oxnard, California, and my mom would watch me walk down a block to go to kindergarten! He was acting like my mother. She would have really loved him! When I got to Lisa's house, I turned and waved to Mother Hen.

Lisa was an outstanding hostess, and she was a Christian! *"Thank You, God!"* I was hoping we would become good friends, and we did. Lisa and her husband, Ed were wonderful people, and even better Christians. They had a lovely family and we would end up spending a lot of time with Lisa and Ed, and even with their extended family. God had come through again! I had finally confessed to Lisa my health problems.

She became my angel. A lot of well-meaning people will say, "Tell me if there is anything that I can do for you." Don't get me wrong; they mean the offer very sincerely, but most people don't want to impose on your kind offer. Lisa didn't ask, she just did! She would bring over plates of food, knowing that I was unable to cook. She offered her services for anything that I needed. She could not have been a kinder and lovelier friend and Christian. I was truly blessed. Ron, too, was blessed, as Lisa was an incredible cook! It had been two months since I discharged myself from the hospital, and all that I could tolerate were protein shakes. I was so hungry for food, but I just couldn't swallow anything yet. I envied Ron while he ate Lisa's cooking.

When Ron was at work, Lisa would ask me over just to give me a change of scenery. Like Ron, my Mother Hen, Lisa would stand out in the yard and watch me walk over. Sometimes I would just sit in her kitchen as she cooked. Other times I would sit in her den and cry as the fear washed over me like a tidal wave. I could open up to Lisa, whereas I tried to hide my emotions from Ronbo. Lisa and Ed both had the perfect mix of compassion and an undying faith in our Lord. I can't tell you how many times they would pray for me and hold me when I was crying. I don't know what I would have done without them. *"Thank You God for giving us just the right neighbors, again."* Lisa even offered her day off to take me on little "road trips" to get me out of the house and show me the beauty of Maryland. I was always too tired to take her up on this generous and loving offer, but I'll never forget it.

Sometimes I would dwell on the grace and mercy from my loving God. He had put us in just the right homes every time. "He looked beyond my faults and saw my need!" All the years I had sung these words while growing up, I never knew how much it would apply to me! God was making Himself so real to me. I depended on Him like a child does a parent. But, my faith was about to be shaken to the core.

Satan was gearing up for a fight, and I was not able to pray like I should. This is where all my friends took over and carried the burden for me. If it hadn't been for my prayer team all over the world, I don't know if I could have survived on my own.

My precious mother, Shirley Chromeenes Zachary

This is me with my Miracle Dog, Tinker

Our Bichon Frise, Mia Valentine.

My husband from God, Dr. Ron Arnold

Baby Mason at three-months old.

My time as a college professor.

Repairing one of my football players.

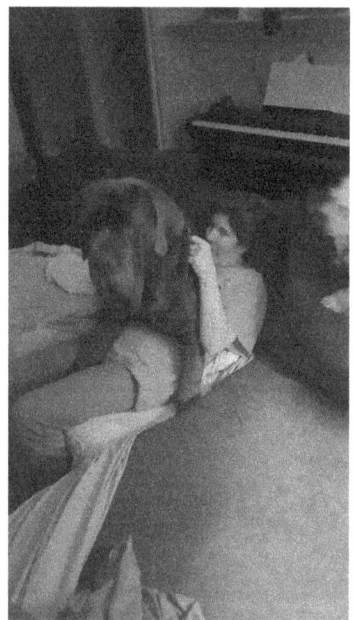

I spent all my days on the sofa with the dogs keeping me company.

Mimi comforts me.

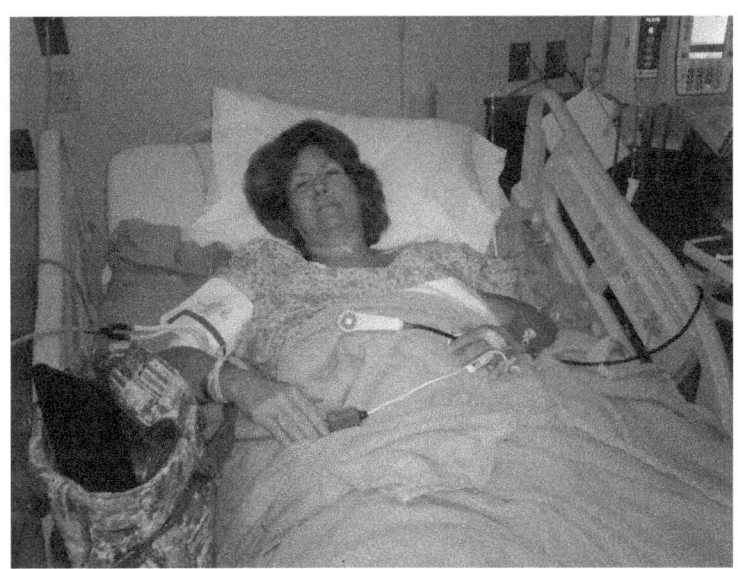

A picture of me in the hospital

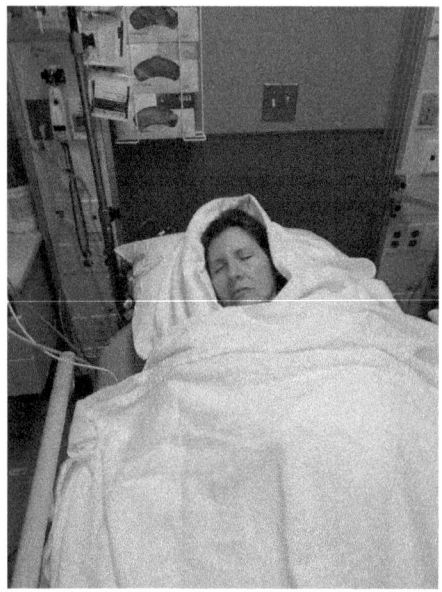

I was wrapped up like a "mummy" in the hospital.

Our adopted Cockatiel, Beaky, and her first Christmas.

*Last Christmas together---What should have been
the last Arnold family Christmas Photo.*

My favorite picture of Ron and Mimi!

Ron went all out on what should have been my last Valentine's Day.

Where I was standing when I was healed. Holy ground!

My 'first' birthday 8 days after my healing. I had a lot to smile about!

*When Ron and I went with Ed and Lisa Gordon
to see the gardens in Pennsylvania.*

Right after I was healed, Ron and I went to Ocean City, MD to watch the Navy Blue Angels and ride bikes on the boardwalk.

Leaving for my first speaking engagement at Pastor Darrell and Jane Rose's church. Happy and healthy!

Bob Lubell taped me giving my testimony for his Internet Video Ministry, ComeOnLetsGo. com. An incredible friend and man of God.

Shortly after my healing I was able to attend the 100th Gala for Aberdeen Proving Grounds with my husband Ron.

Pastors Jerry and Ann Price and me on the day I gave my testimony at our Church. A love that has spanned over 40 years!

15

THE THANKSGIVING HOLIDAYS

In October, we had adopted another "kid." Beaky was a white Cockatiel who had come from an abusive home. She had been kept covered up and didn't have any sunlight. We put her cage in the den right in front of a window. She would hiss and try to bite if we got near her cage. I had heard that if you cover their cages at night it will help them feel secure, but when Ron or I would try to cover her, she would start freaking out and trying to bite at the blanket. After several weeks of this, I decided to do what I thought was best and get rid of the blanket. Beaky started to improve after that. We also bought her a treat called "Honey Sticks," and she became addicted to them. She had never had treats before. We soon fell in love with the little bird. Oddly enough, Beaky and Mason became fast friends! A Cockatiel and a Neapolitan Mastiff, quite the odd couple! Ron and I came home one day to find Mimi, Mason and Beaky playing together on the floor in the sunroom! I wish I had my camera out at that moment!

During the month of November, I really wasn't feeling well. Through the help of friends, we were supplied with an enormous Thanksgiving Dinner. I had begun to eat small bites, so it was with great thanks and appreciation that we asked the blessing that day. God was so good, and the family of God had really come through for us. But I could tell my condition was deteriorating. If I rolled over in bed at night, my heart would start pounding as it tried to compensate for the lack of oxygen, and my breathing became more labored. It was now getting where I had to sleep in the recliner, because the moment I laid down, my heart rate soared. Was it really going to get where I couldn't sleep in bed with my husband? Years ago, we had gotten to the point where we couldn't sleep without the other in bed. Even if one of us took a nap, the other was lying down as well. We might be reading, listening to music or watching T.V., but we were together. Slowly, everything that was important to us was being taken away.

The electric grand piano that Ron had bought for me last Christmas had begun to gather dust. I had just gotten where I could play again after an almost 30-year hiatus. That was really hard to accept. Playing the piano had always been an outlet for me, as well as a great source of pleasure. Now to have that taken away after less than a year seemed to be cruel beyond belief. I didn't have many things that I could do, and now I couldn't even sit at the piano and play to the glory of God.

What hurt me the most was that I was not able to do the things that I had taken for granted. I couldn't go shopping without my husband. He kept encouraging me to use one of the motorized carts, but my pride was too great. Only old people used those carts. Whenever I exerted myself, showering, walking upstairs, trying to cook, I would become pale, cold and clammy. Then I became short of breath. The day that it really hit home, Ron and I were in church, standing and singing during the worship service. I had to sit down and get a Nitro pill and put it under my tongue. I was trying to be discreet, but Ron was watching me. "Honey, are you okay?"

It entered my mind to lie to him, but I couldn't. "No, I'm not." He asked me if I needed to leave, but I refused to do that. I wasn't going to give Satan that victory.

I had now gotten to where I could no longer stand and sing. I barely had enough breath to sing as it was, but I was going to give it my best effort. One way or another I was going to worship my Lord! My beloved husband would sit beside me so I didn't feel like a sore thumb sticking out. When I think back to all he did for me, I am truly humbled and blessed. He was the husband for whom I had prayed. The husband that God gave me against all odds had turned out to be a gem. *"God, how can I ever thank You?"*

The day after Thanksgiving, we had decorated the house for Christmas, and it was beautiful! I did what I could, and the rest of the time I gave Ronbo directions on where to put everything. On the times that we disagreed on the placement of a decoration, I gave in to my husband, because how many husbands would do what he was doing? He did all this without complaining. To be honest, he was a better person than I was.

I was looking forward to our first Christmas back East. We had gone out to cut down a Christmas tree. I was struggling to walk, but I was determined I was going to do this with my husband. It was a lovely night at the Christmas tree farm, and it ended up with us drinking hot cocoa by the bonfire outside. I wouldn't trade that memory for anything. It was very sweet, loving and poignant for both of us. The thought came to mind, *"God, will this be my last Christmas?"* I was going to make the most of it.

Several days later, I was in the kitchen thinking about what I could make for Christmas. Ron has the biggest sweet tooth ever, and from what I've heard, he got it naturally from his father. I had been looking at a cookbook that I kept all my favorites in and I was narrowing down the possibilities. I was content to look at all my old favorites that I had made all my life. Ron was in the den watching T.V. Things were good and regardless of all the problems, I had been blessed more than I deserved. Within a few moments, I suddenly had sweat pouring down my face and I couldn't breathe. I sat down on a stool at the kitchen bar. The room was spinning. Something was terribly wrong. "Ron, I'm in trouble."

Ron knows that I only ask for help when I have no other options. My mother called me stubborn. I called it determined. Ron came running at my words and took one look at me and panicked. "Kel, you're white as a ghost!"

Not quite the description I wanted to hear, but he was honest. Ron helped me to the sofa in the den, and I laid down. I took sublingual Nitro and put it under my tongue. I checked my pulse and couldn't find it. I have always been able to find my pulse when no one else could. I tried the radial pulses in both wrists and then both of my carotid pulses, but there wasn't anything. Nothing at all. Calmly, I told Ron that I couldn't get a pulse. He had been trained as a First Responder in the Navy, so he tried to find a pulse, but he couldn't find one either... anywhere!

"I'm going to call an ambulance." I didn't want that. I knew my heart was beating, because I was still breathing, but it wasn't beating strong enough to register. "Okay, then I'm taking you to the hospital!" Once again, the *voice of authority* rang strong. He wouldn't even let me pack a bag. He grabbed my cell phone and my purse and half-carried me out to the car.

It was getting to where I knew all the staff at the hospital. They took me back and began hooking me up to an I.V, heart monitor, oxygen… everything. The doctor came in with the news, "Doctor, you're in severe heart failure, and you've had a heart attack. I need to admit you right away." This is not happening to me! It's Christmas time! "God, I want to be home with my family! Don't do this to me! Please…"

I got angry. *"Satan, I've read the Book, and I know how this is going to play out and let me tell you something, you've already lost the battle! I don't know why you want me so badly, but my God is in control and it's not over until He says it's over! And in the Name of Jesus, leave me and my family alone!"*

I was greeted by name when I got to the floor. I would have cried, but I didn't have the strength. This time Ron's cell number was written on the board in my room. We weren't taking any chances. After Ron left, I wondered why my favorite nurse, Karen, would come racing into my room, only to look at me and turn around and leave. After this happened several times, I demanded to know if she had lost her mind. "Kelly, I'm carrying your heart monitor on me, and it keeps showing that you are in asystole." This means that the monitor was showing that I was in cardiac arrest with no discernible electrical activity on the EKG monitor. Karen always was straight with me, and I appreciated that. No wonder she was tearing into my room.

The doctor came back to check me and told me that my cardiac function was so faint, it wasn't even registering on the monitor. "We've had to reset the parameters for you. Doctor, your heart is barely functioning. Your heart is failing. I'm sorry. I've scheduled you for another Echocardiogram in the morning." He turned and walked out, leaving me to talk to God.

"God, I can't keep doing this. I'm scared and I'm tired.

*"But He was wounded for our transgressions, He was bruised for our iniquities; The chastisement for our peace was upon Him, **And by His stripes we are healed.**"* Isaiah 53:6 NKJV *"And in His name, I'm claiming that healing!"*

I didn't tell Ron. Let him have some more time before he gets slammed with this.

It was at this time that God led me to introduce a Christian artist and a very special song to my husband. "Honey, I have a song I want you to listen to. I think you are really going to like it. It has gotten me through some tough times in the past." I turned on *Through the Fire* performed by Jason Crabb. Ronbo listened intently to the words,

He never promised that the cross would not get heavy
and the hill would not be hard to climb.
He never offered our victories without fighting
But he said help would always come in time.
Just remember when you're standing in the valley of decision
and the adversary says give in.
Just hold on, our Lord will show up
And he will take you through the fire again.

I looked over at my husband and saw the tears in his eyes. When the song was over, he quietly asked me to play it again. It would be later on that I would find out that Ron would listen to the song over and over every day at work. He was able to put on headphones and listen to his music, and this had become his favorite song. *"Thank You God for impressing on my heart the need to share this song with Ron."*

Later on, Ron confessed to me that the only thing that got him through his struggle was listening to all of Jason Crabb's music while at work. And of course, especially *Through The Fire,* because it was like it had been personally written for our situation. I was so grateful that this music spoke to my husband and gave him some comfort, in a comfortless time.

16

IS THIS OUR LAST CHRISTMAS TOGETHER?

I got home from the hospital in time for Christmas.

I was very thankful for online shopping, because there was no way I could get out to shop. The only time I went out shopping was to keep our family tradition, getting a new ornament together and getting each of the kids one as well. That was a really hard day for us, because even though we didn't bring it up, we were both wondering if this was our last ornament as husband and wife. The ornament that we picked for ourselves showed a couple cutting down a Christmas tree. When we looked at it, we didn't say a word. Ron just took it, knowing that we couldn't have asked for a better ornament. Words weren't necessary, and I don't think we could have spoken anyway. We were both choking down the tears.

Ron would baby me any way he could. I wasn't ever really able to eat much, because if I did, it would compress my diaphragm, and I couldn't breathe. However, sometimes I just really wanted the one food that appealed to me, and Ron was always willing to oblige me. I wanted to go to IHOP and get pancakes! Sometimes for breakfast and sometimes for dinner, but Ron never complained. He always just said, "Well, come on! What are you waiting for?" We even had a favorite waiter who knew exactly what I wanted: an order of pancakes and a large glass of cold milk!

Through social media, we had been requesting prayers from all our friends. People all over the world were praying for my heart. I appreciated each person who prayed for me. I was having trouble praying for myself, and I learned to lean on fellow Christians to carry the load for me. I am very thankful for each and every Prayer Warrior I had.

By Christmas, I knew that I was deteriorating quickly. If God didn't intervene, I wasn't going to last much longer. I could no longer sleep on one pillow. I had to have three pillows to prop up on in order to breathe, and when that no longer worked, I went to the recliner. And to my further humiliation, I had to use a motorized cart to get around Wal-Mart. This was just about the last straw. I was going around a corner in the pharmacy when I hit a shelf and brought down an entire display of Depends Undergarments. My face was beet-red. It was not one of my finer moments. I looked around for Ron to help me, but my husband had conveniently disappeared.

After dark, Ronbo and I would bundle up and go for a ride to look at all the beautiful decorations. The town next to us is Bel Air, and it is charming. Little shops on streets all had beautifully decorated street lights. I would have given anything to be able to walk the street with my husband, but we had to be content to just ride around and look at everything. I couldn't help but think back to our first Christmas in Texas. We had sat on the curb in shorts and tee shirts while we watched the Christmas Parade. Even Mimi went with us. Not quite the Norman Rockwell Christmas that we were having now!

It was time to start making some plans, and I didn't know if I had the mental strength to do what I needed to do. I needed to write letters to my three children, my three step-children and my husband. *"God, please give me the strength to do this."* I knew it would tear me up while writing them, but I had to do it. Every time I thought about it, I would start crying. This was going to be the hardest thing I've ever done, but it was also the best gift I could give. So, one day when Ron was at work, I sat down at the computer. I had taken my heart meds, because I knew this was going to be emotional, and I was going to need help getting through it.

My darling Ronbo,

If you are reading this, then I have gone to be with our Lord. I'm writing this, because there are things that I want to tell you, and you know if I had tried to do it in person, we both would end up crying. I know you are hurting right now, and I am so sorry for that, honey. I never wanted you to hurt, but this was inevitable. So, stop crying and just listen to me, okay? You can do this! You are one of the strongest men I've ever met. You left home and joined the Navy when you were only seventeen, and look at how much you have accomplished. I am so proud of you! You've done more in a lifetime than a dozen men.

I loved every single minute with you! You made me laugh; you challenged me in a way that made me grow spiritually, mentally and emotionally. I loved the times we spent playing board games and pushing each other to be better. I never could beat you at Monopoly, but I think you cheated somehow!

I love how you became such a good daddy to Mimi. For a man who didn't like little dogs, you became her protector. My favorite picture is of you and Mimi when we flew from Texas to Washington D.C. You're holding her in your arms, because she had gotten scared from the jet engines, and she wanted Daddy to hold her.

Thank you for the precious years of our marriage. I was so honored to be your wife. I'm sorry I couldn't have been a better wife to you. I loved you more than I can ever express. You are kind, loving and generous to a fault. You babied me way more than I deserved, but I wasn't going to say anything at the time! Ron, you were my rock, my lap on which to crawl when I needed a safe place. I never felt safer or more loved than when I slept wrapped in your arms.

Honey, I know you are thinking that it wasn't enough time, but had we spent a thousand years together, it still wouldn't have been long enough. Thank you for being such a strong Christian husband. Thank you for all the times you made me laugh. Do you remember when I was having a meltdown over having *less than a year to live* and I was hysterically crying and telling you that it wasn't fair? You looked at me and asked, "Do you want me to buy you an ice-cream sundae?" Through my tears, I sniffled, "Yes." And we both laughed, and then you and I went to get a hot fudge sundae. See, you're laughing now, aren't you? Go out and get yourself a hot fudge sundae and laugh while you eat it and remember the good times, okay? Eat one for me while you're at it!

Ronbo, you're going to have some rough times, but with the grace of God you can make it. Stay faithful to God, and He will always be by your side, and He will take you through the fire again! I know this for a fact. Keep listening to that song. It got us though a lot of fires, didn't it? You don't have the luxury of falling apart. Our children are all going to need you to be strong. Both our children and fur babies. Mimi is going to need to sleep with you, and I'm pretty sure you'll enjoy her snuggling to you. Keep some of my clothes around for Mason to carry, okay?

Darling, remember that you promised to not get angry at God. You promised me that you would stay in church and let our church family help you through this. I love you more than I can ever tell you. When I prayed for a husband, I had no idea that God would give me the most incredible husband in the world. You were so much more than what I had asked Him for. Thank you for loving me. Thank you for taking such good care of me. Thank you for loving God and remaining faithful to Him. I haven't left you; I'm just on the other side waiting for the trumpet to sound so that we can meet up in the air… together forever.

Now, my love, go and mourn for a while and then get over it! You're too much fun to stay sad for long. Look at our pictures and laugh at all the private jokes we had! Look at my pictures with joy. We had a love story that should have been made into a book or movie. Most people would think us crazy to get married after a month and a half, but it worked out, didn't it? Tell our children and grandchildren how very much I loved them. Don't let them forget me.

And now it's time for me to go, my love. You have the rest of your life to live and just know this, Ron, *you were so loved*. You were my one true love. *My soulmate.*

All My Love,
Kel

I put the letter with everything that I wanted opened after my death. Then I crawled in bed and sobbed like my heart was broken… which it was. I had gotten it done, and that was the important thing. I don't think I could have done that a second time!

Our 2016 Christmas was very special in a bittersweet way. We went to Christmas Eve Service and stood at the altar holding a lighted candle. My Ronbo put his arm around me and pulled me close, as we sang the Christmas songs I had sung my whole life. It was beautiful and very moving. No one noticed the tears that ran down our faces. *"It took heaven's Spotless Lamb to die for my sins, and His stripes for me to be healed. Thank You God, for the gift of Your precious Son."*

Ron had spoiled me as usual. I felt like a child, sitting under our tree opening presents. I, too, had spoiled Ron via online shopping, but I had managed to get him everything on my list. Mimi, Mason and Beaky made out like bandits! Not only did they have presents under the tree, but their stockings had been filled to overflowing. It, too, was bittersweet watching them play with their new toys. We had found a basketball sized ball for Mason, and he could pick up the whole ball in his mouth! Anything smaller than that, and he could swallow it.

I couldn't bake like I used to do at Christmas. I used to make fudge, candies, bread, the list goes on and on. But not this year. *"God, if this is my last Christmas, it wasn't fair to Ron that I couldn't do anything."* Not only was I sad and scared, but I also had moments of intense anger. I would suddenly break into tears and tell Ron, "It isn't fair! I can't do this! Why did this happen to me of *all* people?" Wow, a little arrogant, don't you think? Illness is not a respecter of people. Did I really just say that I was too good for this to happen to me? *"God, please forgive me. I believe, but please help my unbelief!"* Then the verse in 1 Thessalonians 5:18 came to mind. *"In everything give thanks: for this is the will of God in Christ Jesus concerning you."* Wow. Give thanks for the heart failure that is killing me? *"God, You are asking a lot of me, but I will do it."*

"Then you shall call, and the Lord will answer; You shall cry and He will say, 'Here I am'" Isaiah 58:9 NKJV

New Year's Day rolled around. This is a special day in our home, because it is also Ron's birthday! He was the first baby born on New Year's Day in the great state of Georgia. Normally we would stay up and watch the ball go down in Time's Square, but not this year. I was sleeping for longer periods of time. I would go to bed by 9:00 p.m. and wouldn't wake before 11:30 the next morning. I just couldn't get out of bed any earlier than that. During my years in school, I existed on four hours of sleep a night, and now I'm sleeping over fourteen hours each night.

17

THE TALK WITH RON

We had gone to church that Sunday, but I was having a hard time breathing. For the first time, I had to get up in the middle of the service and leave. Satan had scored a black eye on me with that. My heart ached. It ached like never before. Now I'm losing the ability to go to church.

'Jesus, please don't let this happen. I need to go to church!'

"For I know the thoughts that I think toward you, says the Lord, thoughts of peace and not of evil, to give you a future and a hope. Then you will call upon Me and go and pray to Me, and I will listen to you. And you will seek Me, and find Me, when you search for Me with all your heart. Jeremiah 29:11-13 NKJV

God always knew just what I needed to hear.

Our pastor called us later that day to check on me. He saw that I was having to put my head down to breathe. Ron told him that he didn't know what to say. I had taken three sublingual Nitros, but it hadn't worked like before. My depression was getting bad, and now I had to have "The Talk" with my beloved husband, and it wasn't going to be easy.

"Ronbo, darling, we need to talk." I saw him visibly tighten. "Honey, I love you. I have had the honor of being your wife for six years, and I want you to know that I've never loved anyone like I love you. You are the husband of my dreams, and no matter how much time I have left… it wasn't enough time with you. But know that I will be watching and waiting for you." We both had tears pouring down our faces.

"No, Kel, I don't want to talk like this, I can't handle it!"

My poor love, my darling husband, I don't want to hurt you, but I've got to tell you some things. "Ron, I have to do this. *We* need to talk about "afterwards." Ron was turning his head from me, "I can't do this! I can't lose you, Kel!"

I had to bite the bullet and talk to him anyway. He was never going to be ready for this conversation, but I was running out of time. "Honey, I love you, but we have to have this talk." Ron had turned completely away from me, as if not seeing me made me go away and would silence the words that he dreaded to hear. "When I die, I don't care what you do with my body. Donate it to science, cremate it, or bury it. I want you to do what makes you feel better. I still have my mother's ashes, and it gives me comfort to 'have her around,' but I want you to do what brings you the most comfort. If you want to have me buried in Connecticut next to your son Tyler, then do it. I will have letters for you to give our children and one for you. I have put together a box of things and letters for any grandchildren with whom we might be blessed. There are books I read when I was young that were special to me, and pictures I want them to have." I continued to tell him my wishes, but I knew that I would have to write everything down, because Ron was numb and in shock and was not going to remember anything I told him.

After my mother had died, and I was finally able to muster the strength to go through her things, I found that she had left me gifts that I never knew about. Every time I had gotten her a greeting card for her birthday, Mother's Day, anything, she had written me a note in the card about how she felt about the card or that day. I had no idea she had done that for me all these years! Then one day about a year after she died, I found a letter she had written to me in the small cookbook where I wrote down all my special recipes. It was almost at the end of the cookbook, but *she* had thanked me for all that I had done for her through the years. What I had done for her?! Oh, my goodness… she got that backward. "Mom, it is I who has to thank you! And thank you for this special gift." She knew I would find it when I needed it the most, like the chapters from Job she had written down for me. How did she know?

My mom and I had talked a lot about death, and now I find myself trying to think of things to tell my husband to comfort him and prepare him. It was different with my mother. She had an intense love of God and physics, which she said proved the existence of God. Instead of scientists using it to prove there is no God, it had backfired on them and had proven His existence. Mom was not afraid to die. She would talk about it like some talk about going on their favorite roller coaster. She thought it would be the ultimate experience, and she was not the least bit afraid, because she knew "for her to live is Christ and to die is gain."

Now, how can I show my husband that I'm not afraid to die? Yes, he will suffer and mourn, but only for a season. Joy comes in the morning. If it weren't for my loved ones, I too, would welcome death. I have suffered for a long time. Ron, if only I can convince you of God's love for you, even when He decides to take me. I love you, but He loves you so much more.

"God, what can I do to help him through this? He's going to need support." I had told him that when God took me, he was going to have to depend on others to get through this. I told him to contact Pastor and Sister Price. I contacted our friend David Dahn, the one man that he could really relate to, and I asked David to watch out after him. David, always the Marine, told me I had nothing to worry about, he had Ron's six—military speak for "I've got his back!"

18

MY BODY CAN'T HOLD
UP MUCH LONGER

In the first week of February, I got really sick. I had no resources in which to fight.

"My flesh and my heart fail; But God is the strength of my heart and my portion forever." Psalm 73:26 NKJV

For days I had that pervasive fatigue where I couldn't even get out of bed. I just wanted to lie in bed with no lights or sounds. When Ron would come home, he would do everything in his power to make me eat, but I just couldn't. I would drink as much water as I could, but I knew it wasn't enough. If I had used my head, I would have gone to the emergency room, but I was determined to not give in to this. Then I developed a fever that had threatened to run Ron out of bed. I was burning up and had chills, but he had to throw the blankets off, because the heat coming off of me was about to roast him. Then to make matters worse, I got a runny nose. I offered to move into one of the guest rooms, but my husband can be thickheaded at times. *Wow. Did I really just call my husband thickheaded? Typical "pot and kettle" scenario.*

Ron had gone to work when the final straw broke. I developed explosive diarrhea about forty times in one day. Once again when Ron got home, I had to tell him to take me to the hospital. Ron knew better than to question me. If I ask him to take me to the hospital, it means I should have gone two days ago. I was totally depleted of all energy, and I could no longer fight this. I was wondering if this was when my body would surrender to my inevitable death. My hair had begun to fall out in clumps. I didn't see that one coming. I've always had the thick, curly hair from my Jewish roots.

So, back to the Emergency Room, but this time Ron had to ask for a wheelchair, because I could no longer walk. From the moment I walked in, I knew the game plan. First, I get put on the heart monitor and while someone is getting oxygen on me, another nurse is trying desperately to find a vein. I pointed out my "Go-to Vein" that we use when all others were done in. "Here, use this one, but keep in mind it has a valve in it." I know they appreciated the heads up, because my veins are notoriously bad. One time when I was dehydrated, I was stuck thirteen times before they could get an I.V. in me, and that was through the jugular vein in my neck! I don't freak out easily, but that one did me in. I felt like Frankenstein.

A lab tech was elbowing in to draw labs. The x-ray tech was already on deck, waiting to clear the place and get some films of my chest.

"Doctor Zachary-Arnold, we have to admit you. You are badly dehydrated, and your electrolytes are way too low!" I was too weak to tell him that I already knew that I was dehydrated, and that was the last thing my heart needed. So, back to see my favorite nurses. I was put in Isolation, because they suspected that I had some nasty virus, and they were right. I was playing host to the Norovirus, a highly contagious virus that causes all the above symptoms.

That meant that everyone who came in my room had to gown up and glove up. Needless to say, I didn't get a lot of visitors, but I really wasn't up to it. And then another curveball: Ron was home sick. My poor husband had finally succumbed, and it was ugly. Fortunately, neither of us felt like talking much on the phone. Ron was having to fend for himself and take care of the kids. At least I had room service and clean linen on my bed daily. So, now while I'm being taken care of in a hospital, my husband was sick from a virus he got from me. Sometimes there just isn't an adequate way to say, "I'm sorry." The words seem to get empty after you've said them a thousand times. *Now, after all the times he has taken care of me, I can't even be there for him. I don't think I'm going to be getting the "Wife of The Year" award.*

Yes, now I was having a pity party for myself. But on the bright side, I had new respect for Job and all that he went through. Yet he never cursed his God. Suddenly a verse came to mind;

"Rejoicing in hope, patient in tribulation, continuing steadfastly in prayer"
Romans 12:12 NKJV

That wasn't me at all! I'm ashamed to admit it, but it really wasn't me. I used to be that way, but I wasn't anymore. *"Oh, God, is this why I can't shake this? What have I done? Where did it all go?"* I had stopped rejoicing and being patient in tribulation, and I could barely pray, much less pray steadfastly. *"Oh, my God, what have I done? Please forgive me. Don't give up on me. Just please forgive me for my weakness."* The shame washed over me, as I realized what I had become.

So, I was a guest for a week in the hospital. I got the usual I.V., heart monitor, oxygen, and another Echocardiogram. And because it was a virus, all I could do was ride it out and pray that my heart would hold out. Due to my limited immunity, it took me longer than normal to recover. After a week, I was able to go home. But I had done a lot of introspection while I was confined to bed, and I begged God to forgive a sinner such as I.

We had Valentine reservations at this restaurant in Baltimore that revolved 360 degrees to view the city. I had bought a beautiful dress, and we had really been looking forward to going. I held out hope until the very end, hoping there would be a way for me to make a miraculous recovery. I had even tried praying to God, but even that was getting weak. I was losing hope, and that is not a good thing. I knew there was no way I could make it. It was with a heavy heart that we cancelled the reservations for what may be our last Valentine's Day together.

Our friends, Ed and Lisa Gordon had invited us to go to Pennsylvania to see the world renown Lakewood Gardens. It was hundreds of acres of every type of flower, shrub and tree, known only to God. I wanted to go, but I knew that I wouldn't be able to walk in the front gate, much less tour the gardens. I tried to tell Lisa there was no way I could make it, but she knew that I needed to get out and get my mind off of dying. She countered my every argument with reasonable advice. Lisa told me that they had motorized carts or wheelchairs available. I had already lost all my dignity, so why not? At least I didn't have to worry about knocking over a Depends Garment display. So, I agreed to go.

When it was time to get up and get ready to go, I began to cry. "Baby, what's wrong?" Ron had concern written all over his face.

I wailed, "Ron, I'm just too tired to go!" He held me in his arms and let me cry for a minute, "It's okay, Kel. Lisa and Ed will understand."

Guilt was a constant companion these days. I wanted to do things and interact with people. I had made plans to go to the Ladies Bible Study and a knitting group, but when the day came, I just couldn't get out of bed. Any doctor appointment I had, I made in the afternoon, because I knew there was no way I could get out of bed and go in the morning. I even got tired at home, and after I had been up for a couple hours, I had to go take a nap.

I felt horrible. It was bad enough that my husband had to come home from work and do the shopping, cleaning, cooking and the laundry. He never once complained, even though he was exhausted. And now, I couldn't go on an outing that we had really looked forward to. "Honey, I'm so sorry!" How many times had I said that in the last few months? The guilt I felt was overwhelming me. My poor Ronbo. I said, "Why don't you go without me? I'll be fine. I'll just go to bed and take another nap."

Ron looked intently at me and sadly said, "Honey, I'm not going anywhere without you. It just wouldn't be the same."

I didn't say the words, but I was thinking, *My love, you are going to have to get used to not having me with you. As much as I love you, the day is going to come that I will be gone.* Ron wouldn't budge. My husband, my love, my soulmate was going to stay by my side until the end. I worried about how he was going to make it without me.

"God, he isn't ready to lose me yet. I'm trying to talk to him, but he just won't accept the truth. He's holding on too tight. I'm afraid he is going to fall apart when the time comes. He needs Your strength. Father, I love him more than I knew possible, but I can't leave him until he's ready, and I've tried to get him to talk to me, but he just shuts me out. Please help us!"

I tried to bring it up many times, but Ronbo wasn't ready to hear it. I was running out of time, and I needed to make sure that he was going to be alright. Hebrews 1:14 NIV *"Are not all angels ministering spirits sent to serve those who will inherit salvation?"* Ron's angels are going to be working overtime. *"God, please open Ron's heart and eyes to the truth that is unfolding before us."* My heart was rapidly failing, and my husband was in denial.

"I will not leave you comfortless: I will come to you." John 14:18 NKJV

19

MARCH ROARS IN LIKE A LION

Early in March, Ron and I were sitting in front of a roaring fire in the den, talking as we were most inclined to do. We talked about everything: politics, current events, the Bible. There was nothing that we couldn't discuss. We would talk and laugh for hours. My husband was so sweet and considerate, always asking if I needed anything. When he noticed that my bottle of water was getting low, he'd go get me a fresh one. Our love flourished even more under the duress we both felt. I could see the strain in my Ronbo's eyes. Even though he laughed, his eyes remained sad. Sometimes, I would catch him wiping away the tears. Outwardly, he remained my rock, but I could see past the façade. Ron was hurting, and he was terrified. Even from work, he would call to ask me if I had taken my meds. "Are you drinking water?" The near-death experience in the hospital kept him on top of my water consumption. One day, much to my amusement, I discovered he would count the water bottles in the refrigerator before he left for work. After I finished laughing, I cried. Not a moment went by that I wasn't on his mind. *"God, please help us! He isn't ready to lose me!"*

Ron and I had been married in a civil service, but it had always been our desire to have a proper wedding in our Church. We were going to have a military wedding, complete with a Navy Honor Guard with an arch of Sabers. I had my wedding dress picked out. Ron was going to be in Mess Dress Blues. We had every detail down, except for when we would be stationed in one place long enough to have the wedding. I thought we were going to be able to have it in Shreveport, but that didn't turn out. As my heart deteriorated, I knew that there was no way I was going to be up to having the wedding of my dreams to the man of my dreams.

In anticipation of the wedding, Ron and I had designed an engagement ring and matching wedding bands. Ron was going to replace my current ring with the one that a fantastic jeweler made for us. We had found this charming, little jewelry store in Bel Air, called F & L Jewelers. I fell in love with them. It was a family business owned by Fausto Argueta and his daughters Victoria and Veronica. They were devout Christians who, when they found out about my heart failure and that I didn't have long to live, prayed earnestly for me. They even took the time to have all their employees gather around me in the middle of their store, hold hands and pray for me! You don't find that very often, and it touched me to the core. He understood just what we wanted for the engagement ring, and he put his heart into making it perfect for me. He truly was an artist. I was going to get the new engagement ring right away, but we would save the wedding bands for the wedding.

I had to break the news to Ron that I just wasn't up to planning a wedding, much less going through with it. I thought my heart would break. The wedding had meant so much to both of us, and now I didn't have the strength or the time left on Earth to go through with it. I knew it would mean a lot to Ron to have beautiful wedding pictures to look at after I had died. Score another black eye from Satan.

I was not afraid to die. My sweet mother had been the same way.

"Yea, though I walk through the valley of the shadow of death, I will fear no evil" Psalm 23: 4 NKJV

In fact, she thought that death would be the ultimate adventure. I knew that I would be with our Lord, but I wasn't ready to leave Ron, and he certainly wasn't ready for me to leave him. I can't even imagine the fear he must have felt when he had to perform CPR on me. Knowing that my life was in his hands is not a burden a husband should experience. I know how hard it is having the life of your patient in your hands, but I couldn't fathom how he must have felt.

Many months before, we had flown to Tampa to watch the Navy football game. I was sitting near the window, when I heard the flight attendant announce that they had a medical emergency and needed a doctor. I threw down my book and plowed over Ron and the woman sitting next to him. Here we were, at 30,000 feet and I was responsible for the life of a young man, and the stress was immense. Fortunately, I was able to go into *doctor mode* and distance myself from the situation, but Ron was always in *husband mode*. The stress on Ron was immense, and I could see the toll it was taking. I was helpless and I didn't like the feeling.

We were sitting in front of the fire, talking and just enjoying each other's company, and I began to feel pressure in my chest. This wasn't unusual, but it was getting quite uncomfortable. Ron noticed that I was restless and asked if I was alright. I told him that I was okay, but the truth was that the pain was getting worse than usual. I remembered a song I sang as a child, "Til the storm passes over and the thunder sounds no more, til the clouds roll forever from the sky! Hold me fast let me stand, in the hollow of Your Hand. Keep me safe til the storm passes by." *"Father, please hold me in Your Hand…I'm scared!"*

Soon the discomfort became pain and shortness of breath. "Honey, I need to go to the hospital." Here we go again. The emergency room was packed. As I checked in, I told them that I was having a cardiovascular incident. Doctor speak for "I'm having heart problems and I need to be seen immediately!" Whenever someone presents to the E. R. with these words, it strikes an urgent response and standard protocol says that the patient is taken back immediately for evaluation. I was asked to sit down until I was called. *Seriously? Are you kidding me?*

Ron took my arm and led me to our seats. About fifteen minutes later, I heard my name called, "Dr. Zachary-Arnold?" Finally! We were led into the triage room, where I gave a brief, but vital synopsis of my heart failure and previous heart attacks. The nurse took my vitals and started an I.V. on me. "Okay, you can go have a seat back in the waiting room."

"What?!" I reiterated that I was having chest pain.

"Doctor, I am aware of that, but we don't have any room in back. Just sit down and we'll call you as soon as we can."

Ron was not happy at all, but what could we do? So, we sat and watched the T.V. After about an hour, I got mad and went to the admissions desk, "You do realize what a cardiovascular incident is, don't you?" Yes, I was getting a little sarcastic.

"When we have a room, we'll call you!" This was not the usual hospital I always went to. We decided to try another hospital. To be honest, I was getting embarrassed at all the times I had been to my "usual" hospital. I was getting a little put out, especially when I saw patients walking back, who obviously did not have heart issues!

After two and a half hours, I had all I was going to take. I went into the triage room and asked for a gauze pad and Band-Aid. Unwittingly, the nurse gave them to me, and I walked back to sit by Ron. "Honey, would you hold my phone and glasses?"

Ron took them from me, and then looked over at me and roared, "What *do* you think you're doing?!" Calmly, I told him I was taking out my I.V. and was leaving. My husband grabbed my arm and kept a tight grip on it. I gave Ron a dirty look, but once again, the *voice of authority* had spoken, and wouldn't relinquish my arm! The triage nurse must have heard the roar, because she came out and said, "Come with me, Doctor."

I was mumbling under my breath about calling the Coroner. Now, Ron was giving me a dirty look. "Be nice!" At last, I was taken into a treatment room and a tech came in and gave me an EKG, and another tech drew blood labs on me. Someone else took a chest x-ray. About fifteen minutes later, the doctor walked into my room. "Well, Doctor, it appears you are having a heart attack, and we need to admit you."

Sarcastically I asked "Really?", I looked at Ron and then the doctor. "You have got to be kidding me. This just keeps getting better and better." I was not in a good humor at all, and frankly, after being made to wait for two and a half hours with a heart attack, I didn't care who knew it!

"God, You promised not to put more on me than I could bear, but I'm at my breaking point! I need You! I need Your healing. God, are you listening to me?" I was at a new low point in my life. I was dying and for some reason, God was not healing me. In fact, it was getting so much worse.

I was getting used to the hospital visits. I could have even ordered my own tests, but the doctor would not have been amused. "Good morning, Doctor. Your cardiologist has ordered an Echocardiogram to be performed today." *Wow. Who could have seen that one coming?* As I lost my sense of humor, I used sarcasm as a coping mechanism.

Later on, the doctor came in to give me the results. "I'm afraid I have bad news for you. Doctor, your Tricuspid Valve has developed regurgitation." That felt like a sucker punch. Two of my four valves had regurgitation. *Oh, my God! I'm really going to die, aren't I?* The doctor walked to the door and turned around. "I'm sorry, Kelly. I can't imagine what you are going through." That was the understatement of the year. Fortunately, Ronbo was at work, and if I could help it he was not going to hear the latest development. I buried my head in my pillow and pretended I was sleeping, while I sobbed like a baby. *"God, where are You? You said you would never leave or desert me, but I can't feel You! God, please help me. Help Ron prepare for my death."*

20

PAX RIVER NAVAL AIR STATION

I lay in the hospital bed, thinking about the past. When you're in the hospital and really sick, all you can really do is think. And my mind went to the past. When I was a teenager, we were transferred to Patuxent River Naval Air Station in Lexington Park, Maryland. As soon as we got there, my mom began looking for a Church of God or even an Assembly of God, but there were none in the area.

My mother became very depressed. Her relationship with God and being able to go to church three times a week was the only thing that kept her sane while she was married to my father. So, my mother started a Church of God in our living room!

Looking back at it now, I don't even know how she did it. How did she find people who wanted to attend church in our living room? But she did it! And it was awe inspiring how quickly the church grew.

"I was glad when they said to me, Let us go into the house of the Lord" NKJV Psalm 122:1

From there we went to having services in a store front. It wasn't long before God blessed us with the money to buy property and put a trailer on it. We were so happy to have a "real" place to worship. We had Quonset Huts outside for Sunday School classes. It may have just been a trailer, but try telling that to the Holy Spirit! Most every Sunday night was spent with everyone crowded at the altar, worshiping and praising our Lord God, the Alpha and Omega! My mother was the church pianist, so we were there until the doors closed. It was during this time, I began playing for the church too. I mainly played for the choir and for special singing. My mom and I would swap off to give each other a break. I loved every minute of it!

Soon we heard that we were getting a new pastor. The church was overjoyed! We were all standing around outside, anxiously waiting for Pastor Jerry and Ann Price and their adorable little girl, Missy, to drive into the parking lot. They were young, but I had never—even to this day—heard a better pastor. He was on fire for the Lord, and Sister Ann was the sweetest, prettiest pastor's wife I had ever seen. I became very close to them. Pastor led the choir, and he and Sister Ann sang together, so I spent a lot of time with them, playing the piano. I babysat for Missy on Tuesday nights, while Sister Ann went to the ladies prayer meeting. Missy, who was about two-years old, was the first child I ever babysat, and I fell in love with her! I would give her a bath, and then we'd go sit on her parents' bed and watch Happy Days and M*A*S*H. Missy would start dancing as soon as she heard the music to Happy Days! Through social media, I was able to find them, and it was like finding long lost family! I can't imagine the joy "When We All Get to Heaven."

I enjoyed spending time around Pastor Price and Sister Ann. My father had been very abusive for as long as I could remember. He and my mom did not have a good marriage. My mom was a Christian, but my father was far from it. So, the only example I had as a teenager of a loving, Christian marriage came from watching the Prices. They will never know the impact they had on my life in their example. They weren't much older than I was, but they were so mature and grounded in their love of God and each other. I loved watching them!

I remember one night when I had gone over to babysit Missy. Sister Price had gone to the ladies' prayer meeting, and Pastor was cleaning up the kitchen after dinner. I had never seen my father do that for my mom, and curious, I asked Pastor why he was doing that. Isn't that what wives are supposed to do? Pastor explained, "Well, I figure if my wife can do all the work in preparing the meal, the least I can do is clean the kitchen." I'm pretty sure that Pastor wouldn't remember giving me that explanation, but it really made an impression on me. I decided that I wanted a husband just like Pastor—a loving Christian, and a man who loved his wife as Paul had instructed the Church in Ephesians 5:22-33.

Sister Ann would show me how a Christian wife should honor her husband. Through the years, I would often refer to their example and try to emulate the loving marriage they had. I had never heard them raise their voice at each other or make a rude remark. Pastor Price treated her like she was a china doll, and she treated him like he was her answer to prayer. I loved them so much!

Eventually, the Church was able to raise the money to build a beautiful sanctuary. It was with tremendous pride that my mom and I watched as the new piano was rolled into the sanctuary. It was there that I began to play "My Tribute" written by our family friend, Andrae Crouch, as Pastor led the choir and sang the solo for that song. It became special to me in a very intimate way that would affect the rest of my life. I loved that church and the Prices became my pastors for life!

Pastor Price carries the distinction of being the person who had embarrassed me more than any living person has ever done. And to make it worse, it was all my fault! I was your typical teenager, and there was a teenage boy at church whom I had a crush on. One day all the congregation was at the church for a bake sale. I had gone inside the church and saw my young man, who then invited me into the storage room. We were standing there kissing, when the door suddenly opened, and Pastor Price stood staring at us! "Kelly!" I knew for sure the roar from Pastor had just alerted the entire Church. *"Please, God, just let the floor swallow me whole!"* He stood shaking his head at us, while I had turned a painfully dark shade of red. My face was burning. "I can't believe I just found my piano player in the closet kissing a boy!" I just wanted to die. Did he have to twist the dagger in my heart? My beloved Pastor had just caught me in a compromising situation, which embarrassed me beyond belief! I slunk out of the storage room, trying to avoid eye contact with Pastor Price. I don't remember how long it was before I could look at him without turning scarlet. I wonder if he still remembers that day? I really hope not, because I still get embarrassed thinking about it!

When I started having heart problems, the first people I told were the Prices. I've had some incredible pastors through the years, like Pastor Larry Burton at the Jacksonville, Arkansas Assembly of God. He had shown up at the hospital when my mom died and held me in his arms and prayed for me while I cried as I've never cried before. The first time I had ever seen

Pastor Burton and Sister Marilyn, he had hugged me and told me he loved me, something he did to everyone. You just knew that this man of God meant what he said. The congregation would stand in line so they could go out the exit where Pastor Burton was standing. If they were like me, they just wanted to feel the hug and hear the words from his heart, "I love you!"

The next were the pastors at the Shreveport Community Church. And from Hawaii were Pastor Robert Fisher and Sister Mary Fisher. They ended up following us to Maryland where Pastor Fisher was made the Church of God State Overseer.

But the ones I needed to talk to were those who had made such an impression on me at an early age. I called Sister Ann and asked her and Pastor to pray for me. When we had reconnected through social media, it was like finding long lost relatives! We were so happy to catch up. Naturally, they were upset to find my mother had passed away. But when you're in the family of God, you're just waiting for the reunion of all reunions in Heaven! I love having that blessed assurance that we will all be together again.

I found out that Missy worked at her father's church, and Missy had followed in her mother's example and had married Pastor Todd Rigney, who was the assistant pastor at her father's Church, the International Community Church in Frederick, Maryland. As Pastor Price is getting ready to retire, Pastor Todd and Missy are getting ready to step in and take over as lead pastors. I got to talk to my little girl again, but this time she was a pastor's wife and the mother of two boys of her own! I told her about Happy Days and she laughed. She still loves that show, and so do I.

Recently, I had my 40th high school reunion in Pax River, and we were able to go by the church my family started. I stood on the steps alone. Ron knew to give me a little privacy. All the memories came flooding back in. I've been so blessed all my life. To see that the church that we had built filled me with such pride and love, and the memories flowed along with the tears.

Everyone in that church had been so close. My mother had her close friends, Vi and Carol who had sung in a trio. They were laughing and clowning so much, and if my mother got tickled over something humorous, she had a bad habit of being unable to stop laughing. When you got the three of them together, it was a recipe for disaster.

I remember one time, I was sitting on the front row where I could get to the piano when needed. Mom was sitting in the chair behind the piano. You could just see her face and that was how we communicated. This evening, we had a young, on-fire, new preacher by the name of Roger. He was trying to get his feet wet preaching in front of the congregation and Pastor Price had given up the pulpit for the night. Roger was preaching, and what he lacked in experience, he more than made up in enthusiasm! What Roger had meant to say was;

"You need to be willing to lay down your life for a friend," John 15:14 NKJV.

Well, in his exuberance he belted out, "You need to be willing to lay down your *wife* for a friend!" I made the mistake of looking at my mom, who in her hysterics had tears rolling down her face. Then I got tickled and started laughing. If I remember correctly, the entire church was hysterically laughing! Poor Roger. I felt so sorry for him. He was as my husband calls, a ginger. He had red hair and the makings of a beard. The rest of his face had turned scarlet.

One year we had put on a Christmas play that Pastor had written, and it was powerful. I played the Christian daughter of a Christian mother, Sister Ann and her unbeliever husband, played by Pastor Price. In the play, my "parents" and I had gone to bed and when my "father" woke up, the Rapture had taken place, and he had been left behind! I remember that during one rehearsal, some people wandered in to watch, and they gave their hearts to the Lord! It was an incredible play, and we had people running to the altar afterwards. They couldn't get there fast enough! Praise God!

Now that Ron and I had moved back to Maryland, I am only about ninety minutes away from the Prices, and soon I want to go visit with them. They are family, and I couldn't love them more.

I had been discharged to go home. It was with mixed feelings that I walked in the front door once again, only to be assaulted by Mimi and Mason! They were getting as tired as Ron and I were at my constant hospital stays. All I could think was "How many times am I going to go through this?" I never fully unpacked my bag. Hope was dwindling, along with my heart.

"Hope deferred makes the heart sick, but when the desire comes, it is a tree of life" Proverbs 13:12 NKJV

21

IS THIS THE END?

Around the first of March, I came down with a virus. It started out with a runny nose and coughing. I was really wondering what Satan feared about me, because he was trying his best to kill me or just get me to give up. I had pretty much figured out that my last days on earth were going to be spent in bed. I didn't even have the energy to lie on the sofa. I could have written a book on self-pity. I had gotten to the point where I didn't even tell anyone that I was sick again. To be honest, I was afraid people were going to think that I was a hypochondriac. I've had patients who were hypochondriacs, and I've never understood why some people like to be sick.

That was pride getting the best of me. I should have been honest with Lisa and our Church, if only to get some help for my poor husband. Looking back at it now, I had chosen my pride over help for my husband. Wow, was I really that shallow? *"Oh, my God, what is happening to me?"* The guilt I felt weighted me down until all I could do was cry. The upper respiratory symptoms were getting bad, when the virus spread to my G.I. system. Since it was a virus, there wasn't much I could do except keep as hydrated as possible.

I was wondering if death wasn't preferable to what I was going through, not to mention how hard this was on Ron. I didn't say anything to Ron, because I knew what his reaction would be. He didn't need to know that his wife was losing the strength...and the will... to live. I would cry out to God, *"Father, I can't go another minute. How can I live another day like this?"* And then I began losing the strength to even call out to God. I was wondering from a medical perspective what was keeping me alive. Sometimes I would break down and with the little strength I had, I would cry out to my husband, "I can't do this! I can't live like this. I'm going to die and there is nothing that anyone can do about it!" I was having trouble separating my medical knowledge from the knowledge of my Heavenly Father. I was doubting that God was going to heal me. That was a terrible feeling to lose trust in my Lord. I had just been beaten down too long. I don't think I was able to think rationally. Finally, after two weeks I began to recover. Briefly.

"Trust in Him at all times, you people; Pour out your heart before Him; God is a refuge for us." Psalm 62:8 NKJV

On March 26th, during the night I had an annoying cough. It was enough to keep Ron awake. I thought maybe it was allergies. I had been really tired that day. Ronbo left at his usual time of 6:30. By the time I got up at my usual time of 11:30, the cough had gotten worse. NO! I can't do this again! I drove myself to my doctor where I was diagnosed with bronchitis. *Are you kidding me? "God, have you forsaken me? Seriously, I don't have anything left to fight this!"* I got my antibiotic and cough suppressant filled at the pharmacy.

I called Ron when I got home. There was no way I could hide this from him. "Honey, please tell me this is just a bad joke!" *No, my love, however I am beginning to feel like the Satan has a target on me.*

"It's okay, honey. I've got my meds and I'll be fine." I didn't dare tell him how I really felt. It would have scared him. I was terrified!

That night after my husband got home, and we had gone to bed, Satan sucker punched me and got in another black eye. I was really getting tired of him. Why was Satan so dead-set on destroying me? Was I really that big of a threat to him? I was beginning to feel like Job! I began coughing—constantly—every few seconds. I moved to the recliner in our bedroom, because I couldn't lie down and breathe. I couldn't sleep more than a few seconds at a time. This was definitely *not* bronchitis.

Ron went to work that morning. I stayed in the chair all day, only able to sleep for just a few seconds at a time. I couldn't even speak, just cough. When Ron got home that night, I had gone for 24 hours without sleep. Just a constant, never-ending cough. I was seriously coughing every few seconds. I was worn out and I felt sick and heartbroken. Had God forsaken me? I needed to talk to God, but I couldn't. When I tried to pray, I would start crying and it's hard to cough and cry at the same time. Ron had taken one look at me and said, "Come on, I'm taking you to the E.R." This time we went back to my favorite hospital.

This time I was put in a room right away. I was asked if I had traveled out of the country lately. I remember thinking, *are you kidding, I haven't even traveled out of my home!* Anyone who got near me put a mask on, and they made me wear one as well. That didn't go over very well. I felt like I was suffocating. I kept taking it off to get a breath to cough. The respiratory therapist came in to give me a breathing treatment. Blood was drawn, oxygen was given to me and the inevitable EKG. And then someone took my temperature. It was 103 degrees! *What is wrong with me?* The breathing treatment didn't help, and I ended up having to get two more.

The doctor felt sorry for me and gave me a shot for pain so that I could rest. Other patients would walk past my cubicle and look at me with pity in their eyes and tell me they were praying for me. This is bad when other patients are praying for you. This was one of my lowest moments, yet I saw human compassion from fellow patients, virtual strangers and it touched my heart. In the middle of adversity, I was seeing a cohesiveness develop between me and the other patients. However, I was getting really tired of being the patient. I don't even feel like a person any more. Just a patient. Always the patient. I don't remember how it feels to be a doctor…or a wife.

The doctor walked in to give me the news. "Well, Doctor, you just tested positive for Type A Influenza, and you have pneumonia. *Oh, come on! This is not happening to me.* And then she ratted me out to Ron. "How long have you been in liver failure?" I cringed, waiting for the inevitable roar of anger from Ronbo.

The bellow that erupted from my husband could be heard in the entire hospital, "*Liver failure*! When were you going to tell me that you were in liver failure?!" The thought entered my mind to say, "Never," but I figured he was in no mood for that.

Then the doctor twisted the knife in me, "And I see that you have developed Tricuspid Valve Regurgitation from your last Echo." Ron was turning a ghastly shade of green. The doctor asked him if he was getting sick also. He shot me a pointed look and told her that he was just tired.

Yeah, tired of his wife withholding information. Ron was so mad, he was shaking. Maybe it was fear, or a combination of the two.

The doctor walked out, and I began to cry. I was sick, tired and my husband was about to chew me out. "Honey, I'm sorry. I didn't tell you, but I thought it was for your own good. I didn't want to worry you anymore."

He argued with me, "But what if you had died?" Ron was still in denial.

"Honey, I *am* going to die." I had given up on trying to be brave and strong and positive. I was going to die, and I didn't think it would be much longer. I didn't know if I was going to make it through the night. My body was worn and battered, and I was exhausted. I didn't have any reserves left. I had made peace with the fact that death was imminent, now my darling Ronbo needed to make peace with it as well

I had an appointment with one of the leading cardiologists in the country and my appointment was in three weeks. After several weeks, I had eventually recovered from the flu, but it had taken its toll on my body. I spent my days dwelling on God and His grace and mercy. I came to quietly know God on a new level. I had yelled, cried, begged God, and worst of all, I had doubted Him. One day God spoke to me and I heard the words;

"Be still and know that I am God! Psalm 46:10 NKJV It was time for me to go back to the cross.

"At the Cross, At the Cross, where I first saw the Light. And the burden of my heart rolled away. It was there by faith I received my sight. And now I am happy all the day."

What a fitting song for my situation. "Where I first saw the Light and *the burden of my heart* rolled away." I cried when I sang this, but I felt a weight lift off of me. *"My Father, You are the Alpha and Omega, the First and the Last, the Great Physician, and I accept whatever You have deemed to be in my best interest. Not my will, but Thine be done!"* I had finally accepted God's will for my life…or death.

I had gone to bed one night, and when I laid down I felt a constriction in my chest. I began to cough and it was the wet cough of someone with fluid in their lungs. I felt the rales, or bubbling and rattling in my chest. I was in pulmonary edema. *Oh, dear God, this was it. I am in stage IV heart failure.* By now, I had learned not to keep anything from my husband. "Honey, put your hand on my chest and feel this!"

Ron looked at me with panic and fear in his eyes, "I don't need to, I can hear it! What is that?!" And then the three words I really did not want to tell him. I quietly said, "It's pulmonary edema."

Lately, Ron had been getting a crash course in medical terminology. There was a pause as Ron looked puzzled, and then it dawned on him and horror came across his face. "Pulmonary edema?! The thing that will kill you? Wait a minute! Does this mean you are in Stage IV Heart Failure?" My heart was breaking as I looked at my beloved husband. This was going to be so hard on him.

"Yes, honey. I'm in stage IV now." Ron got out of bed and left our bedroom. *"Oh, God, please be with him right now. Make Yourself real to my husband. Bring him comfort, In Jesus' Name I ask this of You."*

I went to find my Ronbo. He was sitting in the den in the dark. I could see the tears on his face. I sat beside him and held him like a child. *"God, if I could only take away his pain."*

Words were not necessary, we both knew what this meant. I didn't have much longer to live. I had made my peace with it, but Ron was still in pain. *"Oh, my God. Oh, my God."* Ron was crying out to his God. He knew that he was about to lose his beloved wife, and it was more than he could handle. Death is always hardest on the loved ones left alone. My heart was breaking for my much-loved husband, but there were no words that could comfort him. I had reached the end of my life and we both knew that I had only weeks left to live. Neither of us slept that night. He held me in his arms and I could feel his chest shaking from the tears he was trying to hide from me.

22

THE CARDIOLOGIST
APPOINTMENT

It was just a few days before the appointment with the cardiologist. Ron was at work and when I woke up, I was tired and irritable. I was still having to sleep sitting up so as to keep the Pulmonary Edema at a minimum, but it was still there. I was taking Lasix to keep my fluid levels down. Now, I was getting horrible leg cramps from the loss of potassium. My doctor prescribed potassium to be taken each night. Still the cramps and contractures would hit me at 3:30 each night. I would pace the bedroom, massage my legs and cry.

I was thinking back on all that Ron and I had gone through to get to this appointment. We had moved from Texas to Louisiana, and just when we found a great doctor, we had been stationed in Maryland. I had really been leaning on Romans 8:26 NKJV

"Likewise, the Spirit also helps in our weaknesses. For we do not know what we should pray for as we ought, but the Spirit Himself makes intercession for us with groanings that cannot be uttered."

I had given up on knowing what to pray for. I was tired, and I had had all of Satan that I could take. He was getting on my last nerve. I tried to remain strong and positive, but it had been wearing thin for a while.

Much to my surprise, one morning I woke up feeling pretty good, so I decided to go to Wal-Mart and get shopping done. As had been drilled into me, I took my cell phone. I had even made up my mind that I wasn't going to use a motorized cart. I was going to do this on my own! I made it to the back of the store when I realized I was in big trouble! I couldn't take another step and I was having Pulmonary Edema. That scared me most of all, knowing that at any minute it could kill me without a moment's notice, and I really didn't want to die in a Wal-Mart. I saw a bench and sat down and called

Ronbo. "Honey, I went shopping, and I'm in trouble." Without missing a beat, Ron asked, "Where are you? I'll be right there." Fortunately, his office is just a few minutes away.

As I sat there waiting for my husband to rescue me, I felt so sorry for myself. I've always been a self-proclaimed "Shopaholic," and now I can't even make it through Wal-Mart. I had felt okay! That's why I decided to surprise my husband and get some shopping done. Now, I've literally been benched. An older woman walked by and asked, "Honey, are you alright?" I gave her a weak smile and said I would be fine.

I thought back to the days when my mom and I would make a day of shopping. We would go to the mall and then every one of our favorite stores. We could make a day of it in just in the mall! It's still hard for me to go in there without her. I couldn't help but think, *"God, am I going to be seeing my precious mother soon?"*

As much as I wanted to see Jesus and thank Him for dying for me to forgive my sins and heal my body, I knew Ron needed me. There is a song where the Christian artist wonders what he will do when he sees Jesus. He wonders if he will dance in praise or fall to his knees, weeping. I know what I'll end up doing. I'll be kneeling at His feet, sobbing in gratitude and shame for the person I had once been. I imagine that the glory of God will be so overwhelming that we'll all be crying as we praise the Spotless Lamb who took away our sins!

I will never forget the relief when I saw my tall, handsome husband's head coming down the aisle. "You sit there and just tell me what you need." I told him of a few items, and as he walked away, I remembered something else. I called out, "Honey!" To my amusement, three older, well-trained men turned and looked at me. Pavlov would have loved this impromptu experiment! I pointed to Ron, "That honey!" With chuckles, the other "Honeys" walked away.

It was later that God would show an important lesson to me from my experience at Wal-Mart. When I was in trouble, I called my husband.

Never did it enter my mind to beg him or that he would not help me. I had a need, I told him of my need, and then I sat back and waited for him to act on my behalf. Isn't it supposed to be like this with God? I should be telling God of my need, and then with the faith I had in my husband, wait for God to meet my need. God took a bad experience to make Himself real to me. *"Thank You, God for the well-deserved lesson."*

The day had finally arrived, and Ron and I drove to see the cardiologist. I must admit I was nervous. I had never met this man before, and I was literally handing him my heart. When he walked in the room, I liked him right away and so did Ron. He was confident, polite, caring and he listened to me. I knew from his last name that he was probably Hindu, but he spoke excellent English and was incredibly knowledgeable. He had already reviewed all my medical records, so he was up to speed on my rather extensive medical history. We talked about the heart failure and then he said to me, "Let's go for a walk." He motioned for Ron to stay where he was.

We walked down the hallway, and he wanted to see how well I could climb a flight of stairs. I climbed the stairs and per my usual, I began to have labored breathing. We got to a second flight and he asked me if I could try to make it. I was struggling to draw in a breath as I climbed the stairs. My chest was hurting, and my heart was pounding. When we got to the landing, he held the door for me and, as I propped against the wall, he proceeded to listen to my heart and take my pulses. Then he looked me in the eyes and said, "Let's talk."

I knew he wanted to be away from Ron to talk doctor-to-doctor. Somehow, he knew that I was trying to protect Ron for as long as I could. "Kelly, I know I don't have to tell you that you are in stage IV heart failure." I looked at him and nodded. I couldn't quite talk yet. "Well, there isn't much I can tell you until we do a heart catherization on you right away, but then

I'll be able to give you some idea of how long you have to live. I know, at the most, you have *less than a year to live,* but until I get in there I won't know how much longer you have. You do need to start preparing your husband for what is going to happen. I don't think he is really onboard with all of this. You need to get your affairs in order, but you already know that."

I knew he was going to say that, but I didn't want to hear it. As a doctor, I had been on the other end of the catherization, and the thought of it scared me. "After seeing how bad you are, I'm ordering both a right heart and left heart catherization." I was holding on to the wall when my knees began to buckle. He grabbed my arm, "Are you alright?"

I assured him I was fine, that my legs were just tired. But, then I decided I needed to be honest with him. "Doc, I'm scared. My mother had a heart attack and died as a result of a botched surgery by a cardiac surgeon. I need to know how will you sedate me? I don't want to be awake for this." He explained that he would use the normal Versed and Fentanyl. I told him that they would have a hard time putting me to sleep with that. "How about if I use Propofol, considering your traumatic history?"

I thanked him and asked two things of him, "Please don't let me wake up during the procedure and please don't let me die." He chuckled and said, "You're going to be fine. I won't let anything happen to you." And for some reason, I knew that he wouldn't let anything happen to me. *"God, just give me Your peace that passes all understanding, for me and for Ronbo- especially for Ronbo."* We knew that he was going to order the catherization, so it wasn't a surprise.

"And the peace of God, which surpasses all understanding, will guard your hearts and minds through Christ Jesus." Philippians 4:8

We went back to Ron and he explained that he was going to do both a right and left heart cath. He told me to get on 81 mg of aspirin daily, and we would be doing the Cath in a few days. He had to schedule an anesthesiologist for my anesthesia. "My nurse will call you with the date."

Ron and I went back home. He had wanted to know what we talked about and I told him that he wanted to see how I did climbing stairs and explain that he wanted to do both a right and left catherization. "When Ignorance is bliss, Tis Folly to Be Wise." My husband was going to find out soon enough. Give him a few more days of ignorance and peace.

We drove home with a strange calmness. The plan was in action now, and we were mission ready. There was no going back. I had one more hurdle to face, the cardiac catherization of both sides of my heart. I wasn't expecting that curveball, but I guess I should have been used to it my now. The catherization would tell us how much time I had left.

"*Thank You God for being with us today. Thank you for this doctor. Give him wisdom and knowledge as we go into the catherization. I surrender to You, my Father, knowing that I am Your child. You see the big picture, and by Your Word I know that all things work together for them who love the Lord.*" I felt a calmness that I hadn't had for years.

"*And we know that all things work together for good to those who love God, to those who are called according to his purpose.* Romans 8:28

"*Lord, I'm ready for anything You see fit for my best interest. I accept Your Will. Please help Ron to accept it as well.*"

23

THE WARM HAND OF GOD

Ron and I spent the next couple days enjoying each other's company. When we were together we were constantly touching each other. Sometimes words weren't necessary, just a touch. Even at night we slept holding hands. We were both thinking of the day when we would no longer be able to touch each other, and it broke our hearts.

We spent every moment talking and touching each other. I tried looking into the eyes that I loved so dearly, but mine would begin to tear over and I would have to look away. At night in bed, we would watch T.V. with my body leaning on his chest. He would have his arms around me, and there was no place I'd rather be. I'd fall asleep in Ronbo's arms, only to awake to the sound of his quiet tears. *Oh, my love. I would give anything if you didn't have to go through this.* But I was grateful that I didn't have to go through it alone. My heart goes out to those who are homeless and die alone.

Our neighbors, Ed and Lisa Gordon had us over so that their entire family could pray for me. Their daughter, Jessy, was a nurse, and she was going to come over to see me after the catherization. Their son Caleb was such an impressive young man. He openly and earnestly prayed for me. Our Church had a special prayer time for me. Friends all over the world were going to God on my behalf. I felt so humbled at the outpouring of love and support from everyone. Even where Ron works, his supervisor told him that, if he needed anything, to just let her know.

I was getting so many calls from our friends and family. My social media had more messages than I could ever answer. It touched me that people would take time out of their busy lives to pray for me.

Friday, April 28th, 2017 began as a beautiful Maryland spring morning. I woke up feeling stronger with an odd sense of peace. I walked outside to take in the beauty that was all around me.

I stood looking at my flowerbeds, and thanking God for His majesty that was so apparent in all I could see. Ron was at work, and I decided to just go for a ride to Bel Air, the town next to Aberdeen Proving Grounds. It is a lovely, quaint little town that looks like it came out of a Thomas Kincaid painting. I felt pretty well, and I just wanted to spend some quiet worship time with God. It can be difficult around our home with a Bichon Frise, Neapolitan Mastiff and a Cockatiel.

Since we had been in Maryland, I hadn't gotten out much on my own, but I was feeling the strong, presence of God in a unique way. I just wanted to get out and drive and praise Him. The need to praise Him was so strong it was tangible, so I told the kids to be good and I grabbed some water and my favorite praise CD's and headed toward Bel Air. I wasn't asking God for anything, I was just singing and praising God for everything He had done in my life. I was so blessed! I could feel the sweet, sweet Spirit of God, as it washed all over me, bringing me peace and the knowledge that God, Who had known me *before* I was in my mother's womb had this under control. I didn't have to do anything else. The battle had already been won! Praise God!

I had just gotten home when my phone rang. It was the nurse calling about my cardiac catherization date. "We will be doing it this Monday, May 1st. You need to be here at 7:00 a.m. and nothing to eat or drink after midnight, but take your aspirin before you come here." Okay, another hurdle we passed. The day of reckoning was Monday. One way or another we would know what the future held for us. I called Ron, and calmly gave him the news.

I stood in our kitchen and I began to quietly cry. In three days, I would know how long I had to live. I suddenly had the urge to call Pastor Jerry and Ann Price and ask them to pray for me. I needed my loved ones. I called Sister Ann and asked her and Pastor to pray for me. She put her phone on speaker and my much-loved Pastor got on the phone with me.

He told me of the power of God's healing grace. I'll never forget how they sounded. Their voices were filled with love and compassion as they spoke to me. Then Pastor and Sister Ann began to pray for me. I could hear the love and urgency in their voices as they prayed. Suddenly, something strange happened. I felt a warm sensation in my heart! I became distracted from Pastor's prayer, and I put my hand over my heart. It was actually quite pleasant. As I put my hand over my heart, I was thinking, *This is really odd.* It felt like someone had poured warm oil around my heart. It lasted about thirty seconds. Pastor finished his prayer for me, and we all exchanged words of love. A love that had been there for over forty years. We hung up with the promise that I would let them know what happened on Monday.

I didn't say anything to them about the warm sensation. For just a little while, I wanted to be alone thinking about what had just happened. Through the years, I've felt many sensations in my heart. Pain, constriction, beating too quickly, and heavy pressure. But never once had I felt a warm or cold sensation in my heart! I was trying to understand what had just happened.

After we hung up, I decided to walk upstairs and get some things done before Monday. I honestly didn't know if I would survive the catherization and I needed to get some things done. As I was climbing the stairs, I realized that for the first time I wasn't out of breath. I went into our bedroom and began straightening up in anticipation of next Monday. Again, I wasn't out of breath, even though I was rushing around. *Hmm. This is curious.* I kept doing my chores and then walked back downstairs, but I felt different. My chest felt lighter. Something was going on! Then it hit me! God had just healed me! I had just experienced the Hand of God on my heart! What else could it have been? I had chills running up and down my arms, as I realized the power in what had taken place! I began crying and praising God, as I tried to wrap my head around the fact that the *King of Kings* had just touched my heart and healed me! The first thing I did was go to my piano and play "My Tribute" by Andrae Crouch. It seemed very fitting at the time. "How can I say thanks for the things You have done for me. Things so undeserved, yet You gave to prove Your love for me."

I knew that no matter what the catherization showed, it didn't matter because the Hand of God had literally touched and healed my heart!

The rest of the afternoon I was still able to walk, climb stairs, and even make the bed and I wasn't getting short of breath. I felt great! I waited for

Ronbo to get home from work. "Honey, God is healing my heart!" I told him about Pastor and Sister Ann praying for me and the amazing warmth I felt in my heart, "Ron, I know it was the Hand of God that I felt around my heart! Ron, I know that I actually felt the Hand of God around my heart! I know it! It couldn't have been anything else!" I was crying as I went on to tell him how I hadn't been short of breath once since that happened. Ron was cautiously optimistic, "That's great, honey! Let's see what happens this weekend."

That night, for the first time in a long time, I slept with only one pillow. I didn't have to prop myself up to breathe! Ron had followed me up the stairs, and normally I would stop mid-way to catch my breath or even sit down before I passed out, but not now! I practically raced up the stairs. I think I was scaring Ron! The rest of the weekend went the same way. I was not having any symptoms at all! I called Lisa to tell her the news, "Lisa, God healed my heart!" I told her what happened, and she rejoiced with me!

On Sunday, we walked over to show her the difference. Lisa and Ed were very surprised at how well I felt. "God is definitely healing your heart!" They could see a difference in how I looked. My color was better, and I was breathing normally! They told me that their daughter, Jessy, would keep tabs on me tomorrow, and if Ron needed anything at all, to call her. I was giddy with joy! I knew God had touched me! Ed and Lisa prayed with Ron and me before we left, but this time the prayer was now one of thanksgiving and joy! It was with tears, hugs and kisses that we left Ed and Lisa, but we were all rejoicing!

Hand-in-hand, Ronbo and I walked across the street to our home. That night, I couldn't sleep. But for the first time, it wasn't from pain or fear. Instead, I just kept praising God! I couldn't thank and praise Him enough! I didn't know exactly what He had done, but I knew He had definitely healed my heart. The Alpha and Omega, the Beginning and the End, the Son of God had performed a miracle on my heart. I was crying that night, but it was tears of joy…not fear!

24

THE DAY OF RECKONING

Monday morning came early, but that was okay. I hadn't slept last night. I had too much praise welling up inside of me. I had to praise Him. or I was going to burst! We had to get up at 4:00 a.m. to get ready and face the traffic. I still felt wonderful! And for someone who normally had to sleep until 11:30, I was doing great! We got to the hospital and checked in. I was anxious, but only because the thought of someone running a wire into my heart really freaked me out! As we sat in the preop area, I was calmer than I expected, but I did begin to feel nostalgic.

My mind went back to October 1, 2007 when my mother had her heart attack and had to have a cardiac catherization. I wondered if she had been afraid. If she had been, she sure didn't show it. She always had my best interest at heart, so she had been telling me that she was fine and for me to just go home to our dog and come back in the morning. I felt a unique closeness to my mother as we were now sharing the same cardiac problems.

Two weeks before my mom died, she was talking to me about death and how exciting it must be for a Christian. She had gone on and on about how it had to be the ultimate experience. Finally, something I didn't do often happened, I snapped at my mom, "Mother, I know you look forward to it, but can you please postpone it for a while? I'm not ready to lose you!" Mom had smiled at me and said, "I love you, Kelly Girl!" I told her that I loved her too, but I was trying hard not to choke up. Little did I know that my precious mother would die two weeks later. I put away the memories to spend time with my Ronbo.

My husband did something very special for me, he took his cell phone and played "our song", "Through the Fire" performed by Jason Crabb. This song was destined to forever touch our lives. We held hands as we listened to the song that had made such a difference in my husband's life.

There was suddenly a knock and the curtain was pulled back. "Okay, Doctor Zachary-Arnold, are you ready to do this?" My beloved husband leaned over me and looked into my eyes and smiled. "You're going to do great, Kel. God has already taken care of your heart." He kissed me, and said, "Just remember the warm Hand of God!" And off I rolled to the cardiac catherization Lab.

Once again, I was hooked up to cardiac monitors, oxygen saturation monitor, and a blood pressure monitor. I looked like I was getting hooked up to go into space. Someone placed an oxygen mask on me. I asked the anesthesiologist to let me know before he gave me the meds to put me under. Once a doctor, always a doctor, I like knowing what is going on. He agreed, but I don't recall him saying anything. I think he had just slipped it to me! I was joking with the staff, but I did remind the anesthesiologist to keep me asleep! The last thing I remember were the words from "Through the Fire': "…. just hold on, our Lord will show up and He will take you through the fire again."

"Wake up, Doctor, we're through, and you did great!" I didn't feel like I did great. My heart felt like it had just been skewered, and my leg and abdomen hurt!

I managed to whisper, "I'm hurting." The nurse was prepared and brought some pain medicine, so it was just a matter of moments before I began to feel relief.

"Kelly, it's me, Jessy. You're doing great! I just called Ron and told him I was with you." It really touched me that she would take the time to come see me. "I'm going to let you sleep now, but I'll see you later." Her face blurred out of my vision…

I was becoming more coherent now. I could understand what people were saying. A nurse brought me some ice chips to suck on, and I was very grateful for the small act of kindness. My mouth was as dry as the Mojave Desert, where I had been born. I kept waiting for my doctor to come in and talk to me. He had promised me that he would be there, so I was wondering what could have happened. I was just about to go back to the room when my doctor stuck his head in and asked if I was able to talk to him yet. "Yeah, I'm groggy, but I can talk."

The doctor came over to me and just stared at me. I was beginning to think he had horrible news to tell me, and just couldn't get the nerve to say it. And then he began to pace the small recovery room. He was obviously struggling to speak. "This can't be good," I thought.

Finally, he came over to my gurney. "I'm sorry I took so long, but I wanted to go over your medical records one more time." *So, that's what took so long.*

"Doctor, you were diagnosed with stage IV heart failure and given *less than a year to live.* You developed Mitral Valve Regurgitation, *and* Tricuspid Valve Regurgitation. You were diagnosed with Atrial Fibrillation and Supraventricular Tachycardia. You developed Pulmonary Edema, which is very deadly. And you've had three heart attacks. This has all been confirmed by four Echocardiograms and nine different doctors. I know, because I just came back from looking at all your medical records again, and I counted them myself."

I was wondering why he had just read off my entire cardiac history to me. I already knew all this had happened, and he knew that! What was up with him? He stopped talking and began to pace the room again. "We just did a right heart and left heart catherization on you." Again, with the pause… "I don't know how to say this, but we could not find anything wrong with your heart! We can't find the Diastolic Dysfunction Heart Failure, and you were in *Stage IV*! We can't find any sign that your Mitral Valve *and* your Tricuspid Valve were regurgitating. We can't even see any sign that you've *ever* had a heart attack, much less three!"

He began to pace again, "There is *nothing* wrong with your heart and we have *no* medical explanation for this! I cannot explain it. No one can! We even did extra testing just to make sure! We even checked your liver failure, pancreas and kidney failure and they are all fine. There is no medical explanation for what we found. It's like there is a new heart in your chest! This poor doctor was really having trouble wrapping his head around this, and it was really going to blow his mind when I tell him what happened! Maybe I should get him to sit down. I wonder if I should call for a nurse?

"Well, Doctor, I *can* explain it. Last Friday, April 28th, my Pastor, Jerry Price and his wife Ann were praying for God to heal me, when I felt a warm sensation in my heart. From that moment on, I have had no symptoms, problems or anything wrong with my heart! My God healed my heart! I'm not getting short of breath, even when I climb the stairs repeatedly. I am able to cook and clean. I can even walk all through Wal-Mart without getting short of breath, and I'm not even taking my heart meds!"

The doctor looked at me like I had grown a second head. He started to speak, but all he could do was stutter and fumble around for words. He began to pace around the room again. Finally, he came back and stared long into my eyes, while looking very uncomfortable. I think he was trying to figure out which one of us had lost their mind. Finally, he just looked at me and said, "Well, I guess I'm going to have to go along with that, because we have no medical explanation for what has happened. I was crying tears of joy! My Hindu doctor congratulated me turned and walked out, still shaking his head. All I could do was praise the God of all gods and give Him the glory! He saved my life! My God had commuted my death sentence. I no longer had *less than a year to live*!

It was at this time that Ron came in and heard the news. I was laughing and crying at the same time, "I'm not going to die! I'm not going to die!" Ron was hugging me as I continued to rejoice!

"Honey, you had better keep your voice down, because you are going to start freaking out the other patients!"

I was still crying and laughing, "I'm not going to die! I'm *not* going to die!" About this time Jessy Gordon came back in and she had heard the news. "Jessy, I'm not going to die! God healed my heart!"

Jessy was carefully hugging me and was laughing, "I know, I just heard the news! Congratulations!" Our Lord *had* shown up and He had taken me through the fire, and I'm not going to die! My grave *had* been denied! Satan was slinking away with his tail between his tail and *two* black eyes!

We had to stay in recovery a little longer and then I was taken to a room where they could watch over me for the next couple of hours to make sure my femoral artery didn't start to bleed. Ron had called Ed and Lisa and celebrated our victory with them! God was already touching lives with this miracle. It wouldn't be too long before I would find out how many lives He was going to touch with this!

25
LIFE WITH MY NEW HEART

I went to bed when we got home. They had really worked over my heart and it felt like a Shish Kabob. I took my pain meds and slept most of the day. Whenever I woke, my husband was right at my side, grinning from ear-to-ear. Ronbo was not going to lose his wife! Ron had finally admitted to me that his prayer to God was, "Father, I can't spend the next thirty years without her." A simple prayer from the heart of a grieving husband.

It was then that my husband had a confession for me. "Honey, remember when we were in Shreveport right before Christmas, and you had gotten so sick?" The times were all starting to run together, but I knew basically when he meant. "I was driving to work and suddenly I found myself in the parking lot of our church." Ron stopped talking, and I saw that he was trying to swallow. I looked questioningly at my Ronbo, but it wasn't time to ask questions. So, I just waited until he could continue.

"I called into work and told them I couldn't make it in. My big, strong husband doesn't admit things like this to me. But to his credit, he had waited a year and a half before doing it. "I just found myself sitting out in the car, so I went in and the Christmas Production was rehearsing."

Every year for longer than I can remember, the Shreveport Community Church has put on a Christmas Pageant called "Songs of the Season," and it is worthy of a Broadway production. "I just sat in one of the pews listening to them, and I kept praying to God for Him to heal you, because I couldn't take living without you. Finally, this older man, an usher named Mike, came up and sat beside me and asked me if there was anything he could do for me. I could only shake my head. He started talking to me for over an hour. I can't tell you what he said, but at the time it was just what I needed to hear. *"Thank you, God, for guiding my husband to a place where he could connect with You and gain some peace in his heart."*

I was anxious to get up and give my new heart a "test drive." I was moving slowly, but only because of the pain in my leg where they had threaded the catheter through my femoral artery. May 6th was my birthday, and Lisa and Ed Gordon had thrown an incredible birthday party for me. We had so much to celebrate! Lisa had even made a homemade German Chocolate Cake for me, like my mother used to do every year! What a great friend she had turned out to be. I was so blessed to have her and Ed in our lives!

The next weekend, they had invited us to go to Pennsylvania and see the Lakewood Gardens. This time, it was with great joy and anticipation that we accepted their offer. We even went to dinner first! I will never be able to express my joy at being given a second chance at life! I was filled with praise as the Holy Spirit rose up in me. If I spent the rest of my life praising Him, it still wouldn't be enough.

The Gardens were magnificent; they were another reminder of the glory of God! We walked all over the gardens, for about one and a half miles. To use the restrooms, we had to go down 4 flights of stairs and then back again. Not once did I get short of breath or have chest pain! I was childlike in my joy and amazement at the wondrous creations of my Savior. It was if I was seeing everything for the first time.

It was after midnight when Ed and Lisa dropped us off at our home. The drive had taken about an hour and a half. When Ron gave me a hand to help me out of the car, I had a shock of reality that about knocked me down! While my heart was new, the muscles in my body…not so much. I couldn't straighten up! Remember, I had been pretty much confined to my house for the last few years. *Good job, Kel. You couldn't have anticipated this happening?* I felt so stupid walking into the house like the Hunchback of Notre Dame! I crawled into bed, moaning with each movement. Who would have seen this one coming? The next day was bad, but it had been worth it. I guess God thought I would use the brain He had given me. I could just see God, shaking His head at my stupidity. Okay, it is a little funny!

The weekend of May 28th was my St. Mary's Academy 40th high school reunion. I had reconnected with a lot of the girls via social media. They all knew of my heart failure and my healing. I was so excited to be going and seeing everyone again! Bernadette threw an incredible Garden Party, complete with a *huge* bonfire. Bernadette has this beautiful historical home that she is restoring. I believe it had at least three stories, and I was climbing this magnificent staircase without missing a beat! It would have taken hours to look at everything in her home, but I did the short tour so I could spend time visiting with everyone. Everyone was shocked at the story of my healing, but it gave me a great opportunity to give God the glory and to celebrate!

The next evening was a dinner at a local restaurant on the water. Sharon and Dawn had done a fantastic job of putting the reunion together. Kelly had missed her flight in Texas and drove all the way to southern Maryland! Bless her heart for taking on such a daunting drive. I had really wanted to see her, and I was thrilled that she made it in time for the dinner on the water. I had gotten in touch with one of the nuns at our school, Sr. Angie a couple of days before. She has always meant so much to me, and I was thrilled to find her. I was so happy to share my healing, and my handsome husband with the girls who had been an important part of my life.

So far, I had not stopped moving since my healing! I was loving this! I began to cook for my poor husband, who had put up with his cooking, or microwaved food for the past couple years. I got out a cookbook and began making dinner for my husband. And not just dinners, but gourmet dinners! If I got in the middle of making something and found I was out of an ingredient, I delighted in my new ability to hop in the car and run to the store! Before my healing, the thought of that would have had me in tears. But now, as I was cooking, I would have Gospel music playing and I would be cooking all the while praising God.

I was having an incredible time, and I didn't hear Ronbo complaining! He even had extraordinary leftovers to take for lunch. I was dressing up in the mornings, instead of lying around in my jammies. I was trying new hair styles and tried wearing high heels again. That didn't work out so well and I found myself having to get used to heels a little at a time!

The weekend of June 17th, this Navy Brat and her Navy husband went to the Ocean City Boardwalk to watch our beloved Navy Blue Angels Air

Show! I'm feeling like the most blessed, loved woman ever! I had spent summers at Ocean City when we were stationed at Pax River, and now I was back! Ron bought me a Blue Angels ball cap as a souvenir of my "new life." I often wear the Blue Angels cap while I'm writing.

We even rode bicycles up and down the Boardwalk. The thought went through my mind, "It hasn't been that long that I couldn't do thirty seconds on a stationary bike." I was like a child looking excitedly at everything! I would jump off the bike to go over and inspect something that had caught my attention. Ron had the patience of a saint and occasionally I would catch him laughing at my zeal! I had this overwhelming feeling of love and gratitude for my Savior. "By Your stripes I *was* healed!"

I went down to the ocean's shore and stood looking at the vast water and crashing waves. Nostalgia and joy filled my heart. My heart! My newly healed heart. I had come full circle. Most people remember the first time they saw the ocean, but I don't. It has always been an integral part of my life, as I grew up living on naval bases. The memories came flooding back to me. I was too young to remember, but I had heard the story often how my mom and I were waiting for the aircraft carrier USS Kitty Hawk to pull into port. Per tradition, the Sailors were lined up in what is called, "Manning the Rails." I started crying and was yelling, "Get my daddy off of that ship!" Hey, give some credit to a three-year old who knew better than to call the USS Kitty Hawk a "boat!"

I had even been baptized in the Pacific Ocean, off the coast of Hawaii. For several years I had been wondering if I would ever be able to see the ocean just once more before I died. Now I stood there, in awe of the splendor and majesty of the ocean as tears of joy ran down my cheeks, and as if in a spiritual affirmation of my new life, I stepped into the ocean, only to be promptly knocked down by a wave. Yes, God has a sense of humor! I was baptized once again, but this time it was in the Atlantic Ocean!

26

A VALIANT EFFORT

Not too look long after we got back from Ocean City, I got a call from my cardiologist. "Doctor, I want to ask of a favor from you. Will you consent to having a CT Scan of your heart? I just need to look and see if we missed anything."

Bless his heart, he was really having a hard time with this! I felt like I needed to do this for him to get any closure, "Sure, Doctor. Just give me the day and time." I was scheduled for the next week.

The day for the CT Scan arrived and with some laughter, I drove to the Imaging Center. The only down side was that I had to be NPO, nothing to eat or drink after midnight, because he had ordered the CT with and without contrast. I've got to admit, he's thorough! As I drove there, I prayed. But this time I was praying for the doctor. *Father, I know that You are using my heart to touch the doctor's heart. Please allow him to see You as the source of this miracle.*

I can understand from the doctor's perspective the disparity in what he knew to be scientific evidence of my heart attacks, the heart failure, the pulmonary edema and then the tremendous shock he had when all evidence of it had all disappeared. Even my liver failure had disappeared. He was still trying to rationalize what had happened. I can't blame him for wanting to try one last test. To put his mind to rest that they hadn't missed something, he was going to have to do every test there was to prove one way or another what he had witnessed in my heart.

I wish I could have been a fly on the wall of the Catherization Lab. I can just imagine the doctor picking up the sterile drape to make sure he had the right patient. I wonder what was being said as they were looking for a heart that was failing, only to find a new, healthy heart beating in my chest. Maybe the doctor felt like he was the victim of a bait and switch! Maybe he was wondering if he had gone into the wrong lab.

My imagination runs wild at this point. I can almost hear him telling the staff to reposition the equipment, so he could get a better look. Maybe he asked to repeat the tests to see if the values were still the same. I will never know what went on during my Catherization, but I know that he was really shaken when he came in to talk to me.

It's no wonder he had gone to his office to doublecheck my medical records. I would have done the same thing. I will probably never run into this doctor again, but I'm pretty sure he will *never* forget me. I wonder what went through his head when I calmly explained that *my* God had healed me. He couldn't overlook the fact that a critically ill heart had suddenly turned into a new heart. I wonder if he was thinking about my God? Did the doctor just get a crash course in the power of the King of kings and the Blood Jesus shed on the cross that day? Was he wondering about his own religious beliefs and was he having doubts?

The techs were wonderful as I shared my story with them. They got me hooked up to an I.V. and started the CT Scan. Then they injected the contrast into the I.V. In just a short time, it was over, and I was ready for some food and water! I was starving.

The next morning, I went out to run some errands when my phone rang. It was the doctor with the results of the CT scan. "Doctor, I've been looking over the results of your scan, and I didn't find anything abnormal. Your heart is fine." I told him that I hadn't expected him to find anything abnormal. In a very tentative voice, he asked, "How are you feeling?" It was as if he doubted the validity of the equipment and was afraid that I was going to tell him that I was still having problems.

I told him that I felt great! "In fact, last weekend my husband and I went to Ocean City to see the Blue Angels and we rode bicycles up and down the Boardwalk!"

At this point, the doctor choked and spent a couple moments coughing. When he could finally catch his breath, he rasped, "You did?!" I told him that I've never felt better. "I am able to do anything I want without any shortness of breath, no chest pain, no fatigue…Nothing!" He was silent for so long that

I thought maybe he had hung up, or passed out. I wonder what was going through his mind. He had done his due diligence in treating my heart; it's just that Jesus beat him to the punch. Finally, "Well, I guess there's no reason for you to follow up with me." I thanked him for his kindness and professional work.

As we said good-bye, I said, "Have a blessed day!"

Awkward silence…"Thank you, and you too." I wonder if he picked up my medical records again and went through them, desperately searching for an answer to the questions that were plaguing him. Did he question his god? Did he question the science of medicine? Did he wonder if just maybe my God did exist?

I was smiling, as I drove home. I was reflecting on my life. Through it all, God had been with me all along. Every tear that I shed, every fear I had, He was right there with love and compassion. Even when I had lost everything, like Job, God had restored everything ten-fold. I hadn't lost my mother. She was just waiting for me! God had never forsaken me, He was allowing me to go through the fire to strengthen my weaknesses. And like the three Hebrew children, He had gone through the fire with me! When I look at all that I gained, I am so humbled by His grace and mercy. Once again, the words to "Who Am I?" went through my head. "Who am I that the King would bleed and die for. Who am I that He would pray not My will, but Thine Lord. The answer I may never know, why He ever loved me so. But to that old rugged cross He'd go, For who am I?

When He went to the cross and suffered the pain and humiliation, He paid for my sins and then by His stripes He suffered on His back, I was healed. How can I ever say thanks for all He has done for me? For one thing, I will tell everyone of the miracle that He performed on my heart. It was at this moment that I heard the voice in my head, "*Write a book.*" I had been sharing my story and literally hundreds of people were wanting to hear the whole story. God was using my heart to touch the hearts of believers and unbelievers alike.

I knew the book was coming from God, because on my own I never could have done this! The words were coming to me faster than I could type! The irony was not lost on me, that God had performed the same miracle exactly fifty years ago when he healed my dog Tinker! And the same, identical words had been spoken, "We have no medical explanation for this!" The healing of Tinker had made a believer out of her veterinarian. How much more would God accomplish through my miracle healing? Until my dying day or should the Rapture take place first, I will forever give God the glory, power and praise!

EPILOGUE:
I DIDN'T READ THE FINE PRINT

It has been about 10 months since my healing, and when I look back, it seems like it happened just yesterday. Except for the fact that in these past three months, I've lived a lifetime! I have taken each day and lived it to the max. Daily I thank and praise God for the incredible miracle He gave me.

After years of not feeling well and not being able to do much, I rejoice in being able to do anything that I want! I feel like I've been born again! I'm able to go shopping, go out with friends, and spend quality time with my husband. Someone recently asked me what was my favorite thing to do now. Laughingly, I replied, "Being a wife!" I enjoy cleaning my home and decorating it. I love to plan out meals and shop for them. Whereas before, I had to plan out carefully what I was going to do, because I knew that I only had so much energy in me. I had to take a shower the night before and let my hair air dry, because blow-drying it completely depleted me of my energy reserves. Now, I can shower, dry my hair and get dressed in real clothes *and* still go run around.

I enjoy having dinner on the table when Ronbo walks in. I enjoy fixing his lunch for the next day. The little things that seem so mundane are now very special to me! I am so blessed to feel like "Kelly" again. I've always been fun-loving and playful, and now I am that way again. I enjoy cranking up the music and dancing with our 200-lb Neapolitan Mastiff, Mason!

He loves to dance to Rockin' Robin, and as soon as he hears the song, he comes running. Let me tell you, dancing with Mason takes a perfectly good heart, because he is big and not very light on his feet! But the whole family enjoys our dancing to the song. Mimi is barking non-stop, Beaky is chirping, Mason is jumping and swinging around. Ron stays out of the way and laughs at the madhouse!

Whereas our home always had a pall over it, now it is filled with joyful sounds of life. I am filled with laughter, and I have the playfulness that was my hallmark! Even as I praise Him and joy fills my soul, I will start crying, but this time, it's tears from joy and praise that I just can't seem to adequately express! I laugh and cry at the same time.

In all my years of medicine, I've never seen a patient as sick as I was instantly healed by God. I had heard about miracle healings before, and I knew that my God was able to do it, but to be honest, I didn't feel worthy enough for God to perform such a staggering miracle on me. I wasn't worthy, but God doesn't look at that. The Bible never once says that you have to be worthy to be saved or healed. Jesus died on the cross for you and me. 1 Peter 2:24 NIV says, *"He himself bore our sins"* in His body on the cross, so that we might die to sins and live for righteousness; "by His wounds you have been healed."

There were a lot of days at the end, when I would think, "Is this the day when God calls me home?" I didn't have the physical, emotional or spiritual resources to fight the enemy.

I really thought that Satan was going to win this battle, but God looked down on me and said, No! This is My child and you can't have her! Satan had no choice but to leave me alone and let God heal my heart. When God healed my heart, He also healed my spirit! And now His Spirit rises up in me, and I have to praise Him! The victory was won, Satan was defeated, and I am alive to tell my story.

I had about 4 weeks of a normal life until I heard God tell me to write a book about the miracle He performed on me. I was excited at the prospect, because I love to write. So, for weeks on end I would spend almost 16 hours a day writing. I couldn't rest or sleep until it was done.

Finally, the book was finished, and my life could get back to normal. My poor husband had gone back to eating microwave meals and fast food. But now I could get back to a normal life, however, when God healed me, I didn't read the fine print! Most people are called into the ministry, but I was shot out of a cannon into the deep end of the pool of ministry! Suddenly, people were asking me to come speak and share my testimony. I wasn't an evangelist or public speaker, but here I was speaking to hundreds of thousands of people all over the world.

Then God gave me another shocker; I was to write two more books and share my testimony with younger age groups. This led to the birth of *Kelly's Heart* and *Kelly: The Heart of a Princess*. Now that they are finished, I can finally live a normal life. Yeah, right. My manager called one Saturday to tell me that *Less Than a Year To Live* had gotten the attention of several movie producers and they wanted to begin on it the summer of 2018. Wow! God is so awesome!

I was recently contacted by a pastor outside of Charlotte, N.C. and asked if I would speak at the Mayor's Prayer Breakfast on May 3rd, the National Day of Prayer. In a choked voice I agreed. This was getting to be the big time. At the time of writing this, I will be leaving for the North Carolina tour in about 5 weeks!

I will also be meeting with a doctor who wants to write up my healing for the medical journal!

Every time I talk to someone, I tell them of God's mercy and grace that allowed me to live, so that I could touch lives by telling them of His power and love. Through social media, I have shared my story on a level that was once impossible. Now, I have inherited a ministry. People tell me of their stories of needing God's touch or His healing. They ask me to pray for them, and I am touched by their needs. I had been there, and I knew what it was like to be dying and to cry out for prayer from anyone that would listen to me.

I have been asked to share how I prayed during this trial through the fire. I must admit that there were times…lots of times…that I just cried out and felt sorry for myself.

Isaiah 55:11 says, *"So shall My word be that goes forth from My mouth; It shall not return to Me void, but it will accomplish what I please, and it shall prosper in the thing for which I sent it."* As we believe and confess God's Word we are in agreement with Him for His plan for our lives to happen. That is *powerful!* When Jesus was tempted by Satan for forty days, Jesus would quote His own Word back to Satan!

Through my book I have used Scriptures that were especially compelling to me. I hope you will find them helpful as well.

There is one prayer that I pray often, and I am going to share it now. It has power over any situation in your life; *"Father God, I give my life to You today. You are the Alpha and Omega, the Beginning and the End. I pray blessings on my family and my home. Satan, I rebuke you in the Name of Jesus. You have no authority over me, my family and my home. I rebuke you now in the Name of Jesus by the authority that was given to me when Jesus died on the cross! I've read the Book and I know how this ends for you! So, in the Name of Jesus, I rebuke you from trying to destroy my body. You might as well go back to where you came from! The Bible says that demons tremble at the Name of Jesus and that includes you. I read the last chapter and you have already lost the battle!"*

By just uttering the Name of Jesus, demons *have* to flee. That is powerful! Powerful no matter what your situation is. Pray without ceasing and quote back the Scriptures because they will NOT come back void! And remember that God knows and understands our weaknesses. I wish I could say that I knew all along that God would heal me and all I did was praise Him for the healing that was on the way. I was *scared!* I cried, I panicked, begged, and bargained. God knew, and He understood my weakness and it *was through the fire my weakness was made strong!*

We have a compassionate Savior who knows and has felt every emotion that we have: *"Seeing then that we have a great High Priest who has passed through the heavens, Jesus the Son of God, let us hold fast our confession. For we do not have a High Priest who cannot sympathize with our weaknesses, but was in all points tempted as we are, yet without sin. Let us therefore come boldly to the throne of grace, that we may obtain mercy and find grace to help in time of need."* Hebrews 4:14-16 NKJV

I was able to boldly approach the throne of God and pour my heart out to Him. I could tell Him every fear that had paralyzed my body. I could tell Him my heart's desire and He listened, and He cared! Then it gets better;

"Because he loves me," says the Lord, *"I will rescue him; I will protect him, for he acknowledges my name. He will call upon me, and I will answer him; I will be with him in trouble, I will deliver him and honor him."*

Psalm 91:14-15 NKJV

"Turn to me and have mercy on me,
As You always do to those who love Your Name."

Psalm 119:132 NKJV

I spend my days looking at the promises in the Bible and quoting them back to God, because I knew that His Word would not come back empty. I knew what I needed to do now. I was looking at my Bible like it was a treasure-trove just waiting to be discovered! What a powerful discovery that led to a closer walk with my Savior and the healing of my heart!

I feel by sharing my story, it will show the world that my God is still in the healing business. He is in the miracle business, and no matter your need, nothing is too great for the King of Kings! And most importantly, you don't have to be "worthy". Your sins were erased, and your healing took place when Jesus hung on that Cross for us! And, one day soon, we shall behold Him in all His Glory, Power and Majesty, for our God Reigns!

CPSIA information can be obtained
at www.ICGtesting.com
Printed in the USA
BVHW03*1457300818
526054BV00001B/18/P